I0486740

TEAMWORK:

motivation, commitment and results.

TEAMWORK:

motivation, commitment and results.

RICARDO ZAMORA ENCISO

© 2011, Ricardo Zamora Enciso

Second edition

Original title: "Trabajo en Equipo: motivación, compromiso y resultados."

Translated by Nigel Greenwood

All rights reserved. Partial or total reproduction of this text by any means or procedure, including reprography and computer treatment, as well as the distribution of copies by rental or public loan is strictly prohibited without written authorization from the holders of the copyright, under legally established sanctions.

Please direct any enquiry about this book directly to the author at rzamora@cooplexity.com

Edited by Lulu.com

Cover photograph: www.istockphoto.com

ISBN 978-1-4476-6869-5

This book may be obtained in paper or digital format from: http://stores.lulu.com/RicardoZamora

To María,

without whose company this journey would be meaningless.

Dear reader,

This book is a reduced version of: "Cooplexity. A model of collaboration in complexity for management in times of uncertainty and change".

The original, of a more academic profile, is the result of ten years research and five years gathering data about management behaviour in interdependent environments. The proposed collaboration model called Cooplexity is aimed at developing collaboration teams for improving performance and taking advantage of synergies.

On the other hand, this edition is more accessible for the reader. Logically it does not replace it and cannot due to its size, touch all the subjects of the original work with the same depth and for that reason the quantitative results and, some references to authors or concepts that are more difficult to comprehend have been eliminated.

Cooplexity means cooperation-collaboration in uncertainty and complexity and proposes an evolving model for building collaboration relations. It has been obtained directly from the behaviour of managers with extraordinary results in complex, highly interdependent situations.

It stems from uncertainty, from crisis, from unfamiliarity and goes towards the complexity of strongly interconnected and interdependent relations. All that from a systems and global approach, considering the group as a whole with its own characteristics and differentiated from the sum of the parts. It pays special attention to the cohesion and creation of the necessary conditions for the natural and spontaneous appearance of collaboration. However, not collaboration understood as a renunciation or generosity but rather as obtaining the balance of individual and common benefits thanks to the generation of new options.

Teamwork and distributed leadership are the direct consequences of the model. A model that is strongly supported by rigorous research that has used the Synergy business simulator as a main tool. I do not doubt that even if you have participated in any of the courses using the simulator or not, you will find this book to be a useful tool to apply in your organization.

I will be delighted at receiving any comments or personal experience that the model has evoked and without doubt, all observations because of its being put into practice.

Ricardo Zamora Enciso
www.ricardozamora.com

INDEX

Prologue

With the increase of globalization, complexity in managing current organizations has also increased. This has brought on the necessity for collaboration between individuals to complement each other and improve their results. If isolated individuals are not capable of adequately managing a complex environment, like the current ones, it will be necessary to find other ways of giving adequate answers to those situations.

Throughout my professional career, I have had the opportunity of seeing how the necessity for collaboration has been increasing parallel to the predisposal and capacity for teamwork, within organizations. My first interest then stems from the necessity for verifying the relation between complexity and teamwork.

To carry out this study I have analyzed a series of observations, made over a period of five years from 2002 to 2007, of the behaviour of managers of 52 training courses, given to globalized multinational and large size, internally complex national companies.

The mentioned training course evolves round a simulator with numerical results because of the actions of each group. This allows comparing behaviours with results.

The second goal of this work, from the richness of the data, is to identify the existence of team evolution phases and check if these are empirically validated. Initially I defined an evolution model as a starting point to synthesize the phases through which the groups pass in developing the courses. This model would be finally corrected and replaced by the one herein called Cooplexity.

The simulator, spine column of the training course, is called Synergy as a clear allusion to its goal of developing teamwork. We started to develop it in 1997 and we finished in 1999 after one and a half years of research, design and programming. It is important to highlight that special interest was initially placed in the simulator and as well as the training course, itself to reflect an incipient reality, the increase of departmental cross-collaboration and the necessity of multitask teams. Therefore, the course and the simulator specifically designed to that effect tried more to faithfully reflect the reality than base itself on previous theory. At that moment, I did not know, but that faithfulness would be a fundamental part in the success of the course and the origin of the research and the conclusions reflected herein.

Acknowledgements

Firstly, I would like to thank the Dannon Company and especially Alberto Izaguirre for the confidence placed in my capacity for the development of the Synergy simulator that in later years would become a fundamental part of this text. Even now, when I review the proposal and the original documents, I am still surprised. Pages and pages describing an idea, by means of abstract concepts, formulas, and constant references to the Theory of Systems. Even more so when we are talking of 1996 and the development finished two years later, demonstrating an unthinkable patience nowadays, where short terms too frequently imposes their law.

With the same intensity, I would like to thank Dr. Alberto Gimeno Sandig[1] for his conceptual contribution about the Theory of Systems and the Theory of Complexity among others. Without such contribution, I have no doubts that Synergy would have just become a mere simulator. Even though a magnificent simulator. However, without doubt far from the scope of academic reflection which it could reach, from the capacity of understanding the reality that can be inferred and of the possibility of business projection of the suggested model.

I would also like to thank the people that participated in the design of Synergy helping me in interminable weekly meetings for more than a year and especially Josep Closas Compte from Equus Interactiva, without whose special capacity for landing abstract ideas, it would have been impossible to program a tool of such complexity as the Synergy simulator.

On the other hand, I would like to thank all those multinational companies that have placed their confidence in the quality of the "Teamwork in Complex and Uncertain Environments" course given by Training Games. All of them have contributed to its development and evolution. However, in a special way, for their high level of demand, that stimulated me to give very significant qualitative jumps; I would like to refer, in chronological order, to Agustín Carrasco Eguino and Nieves Márquez de Santos from Red Eléctrica de España, to Antonio Mateo Navarro from Lafarge Cementos and to David Payeras Bailly from Aroba y Ausonia. Also Miguel Angel García Torrente and to Mabel Carabias Costa from the Banco de Santander for their stimulation to start the definite writing of this text.

And in a very significant manner to ESADE as an institution for making space for the seminar among its programs for managers, first as an open course in 2000 and 2001, after as part of the Senior Executive Program, later from Executive Education and currently as part of the Advanced Management Program.

Lastly and not less important, to Joan Manel Batista, director of the Survey Research Centre of ESADE for his un-payable assistance in statistically handling the data with the

---

[1] Dr. Gimeno is professor of Business Policy at ESADE Business School

necessary rigor and approach to solidly establish the final model. In addition, to Manel Peiró Posadas Academic Vice-Dean of ESADE, who from the beginning has guided me in the approach, structure and contents of the present work.

CHAPTER 1

TEAMWORK

1.1 Introduction

Preindustrial society was based on skills. A skilled worker became specialized in a production process covering it from start to finish. He/She accumulated all the information, all the knowledge, all the process. With his/her ability and experience, he/she was capable, with time, of reaching higher levels of development. That knowledge and ability, nevertheless, were personal and costly to transfer. The production process was slow and individualized.

Nowadays, known as the information and knowledge era, technology is universal easily obtainable and little differencing. The product has little margin because competition has squeezed the production processes so much that the solutions have also become common. Fusions, acquisitions, globalization and outsourcing have been adequate answers up to now and during the optimization process.

Therefore, if the internal organization is articulated by projects and the differentiation of organizations depends on their capacity to add value for the end user beyond the product, we rapidly turn to dependence on human teams to achieve results. When machines and standardized processes are no longer capable of adding value to the company offer, the limelight is passed to the people that form it. In fact, we are entering an era where dependence on teams and not on individuals is more and more pronounced. Only multi-disciplined, trained, united, motivated and coordinated teams are capable of managing the interrelations and complexity that affect the different areas of organizations.

1.2 Objective

The present work has the objective of proposing a model that allows developing teams from a functional (efficiency) and emotional (affiliation) point of view. To identify it, I will take the basis of the observations taken during five years in a training course for managers oriented to developing teamwork in organizations. Through game dynamics based on a simulator called Synergy, the participants make decisions in an initially uncertain and ongoing complex environment. From observing the mentioned action of the participants, a behaviour pattern is identified that allows proposing duplicable guidelines.

1.3 Genesis

In 1996 Alberto Izaguirre, then director of training in Dannon España, was looking for training dynamics with the goal of achieving cross-cooperation among the different departments of the company, to improve collaboration. Everybody knows of the communication, cooperation and coordination problems that can arise in departments with different and apparently contrary goals such as the manufacturing and logistics or marketing and sales to mention some classic departments.

The training consultancy company Training Games was then invited to present an offer due to its specialization in creating games and simulators applied to training. This was the motive of the Synergy project, which after one year of design and programming was flamboyantly presented in November 1997. Six months were necessary to adjust the dynamics that were generated with the simulator to training goals. The software was tested and the contents were developed. This way in June 1998, a pilot course was carried out that initiated the first of thirty-five training courses given during 1999 and 2000.

The course became a two-day residential seminar where the participators managed projects making investment decisions with scarce resources. These projects, sometimes interrelated, gave place to group dynamics in which the participants interrelated and took decisions together.

After consolidating the course, in 2001, a process for identifying and standardizing the identifiers of repeatedly seen behaviour commenced. A database was designed for recompiling the information and in January 2002, the observations were systematically registered. Five years later, in January 2007, the period for recompiling data was closed with 52 courses included in the sample. In September 2008, twelve years after the Dannon initiative and ten after the first pilot course, the results of the statistical analysis were provided.

Currently it is still a powerful tool for training and assessment being imparted normally to certain size and complex companies or in the classes of some Business Schools, integrated in programs like the ESADE Advanced Management Program.

1.4 Groups and teams

The first particularity we find is the indistinct use of the terms group and team. In literature, we find this indistinct use between "group" and "team" on numerous occasions referring to the same concept. The difference resides more in the origin of the use than in the meaning that each author gives it. Thus, the use of the term group is more widely used among researchers and academics when they refer to terms like "group cohesion", "group dynamism", "group development", etc. On the other hand, team is used more by those authors linked to organizational behaviour and to management in general, when they refer to "teamwork", "team building", "team effectiveness", "high performance teams", etc.

1.5   Definition of team

When an author wants to differentiate between the most simple and general notions of group-like association, of another more concrete for team, he/she usually refers to the degree of cohesion between its members. Carron and Hausenblas define their study groups as "two or more individuals with a common identity, with common objectives and goals, that share the same destiny, that show structured interaction patterns and ways of communication. They have common perceptions about the structure of the group, they are personal and instrumentally interdependent, they have reciprocal interpersonal attraction and they consider themselves as a group" (Carron & Hausenblas, 1998). Therefore a second important factor appears, as well as cohesion, the common objective. One of the most relevant figures of the Tavistock Institute, Wilfred Ruprecht Bion, in his analysis of groups and referring to the common objective, coined the concept of Work Group especially identifying the objective pursued by the group when carrying out specific tasks (Bion, 1991).

A second definition of team is that offered by Jon Katzenbach who defines it as a "small number of people with complementary abilities, committed to a common purpose, approach and performance objectives, for which they consider to commonly responsible" (Katzenbach & Smith, 1992). In this case, the common purpose inherent to any group has another added dimension, the shared responsibility.

Based on the present text I propose the following definition that has clear contact points with the previous ones:

"A team is a small number of interdependent persons that are spontaneously and naturally coordinated, with the motive of a common project, thanks to a feeling of membership resulting from a determined level of cohesion, making decisions based on shared knowledge".

1.6   Teamwork as a competence

The definition of team starts to become tangible the moment that teamwork is identified as a competence and parameters are established for its measurement. The model of competences has its origin in checking that pure intelligence is not a factor that is correlated to good performance in work and to success in life. Completely to the contrary, the mentioned performance should be measured through such competences (McClelland, 1973). Competence at work is defined as "a subjacent characteristic in a person that is causally related to the effective or higher development in a job" (Boyatzis, 1982). Subjacent characteristic means that the competence is profound and permanently associated to the personality and allows predicting behaviours in a wide range of situations and professional tasks. Causally related, means that a competence causes or predicts behaviour or action.

Competences, as their meaning implies, do not have a universal application. That is to say managing a competence is only sensible in function of a concrete work position in a given company and environment. That way, therefore, although a series of general competences needed by a waiter can be identified, these are modified and are blended in accord to the environment or the company where the mentioned waiter works: the competences needed by a successful waiter in a five-star hotel are not identical to those needed by a "model" waiter in a summer terrace on the coast.

Inspired on the works of David C. McClelland and George O. Klemp, Jr. as well as thanks to the efforts of numerous professionals belonging to the staff of the McBer Company, over the years, the methodology called Job Competence Assessment (JCA) is defined as the basis for complete management of human resources. Boyatzis, identifying the results obtained in different research carried out with the BEI[2] method found that a series of defining competences for professional success existed, independently of the organizational structure and he called them general competences. Due to the success obtained by Boyatzis, years later research was carried out aimed at determining the key competences in employment success that took the form of a dictionary of competences (Spencer & Spencer, 1993). As a consequence of the inclusion of behavioural indicators, each competence ended up being structured around training levels, normally three to six. Each level progressively describes each work competence.

This way the concept of competence is redefined "as a subjacent characteristic in an individual that is causally related with criterion referred to an effective or higher development of a job or situation". Criterion referred to means that the competence really predicts who does better or worse, statistically measured with reference to specific standards or criterion (Spencer & Spencer, 1993).

---

[2] The BEI (Behavioural Event Interview) are a series of interviews carried out on a group of persons that make up the representative sample of "superstars".

CHAPTER 2

REVISION OF CURRENT MODELS

2.1   Introduction

Throughout the years, many investigators have centred their studies both on the dynamics of training teams as on the characteristics of their members.

In this chapter, I will refer to team development or building models as the same thing. I will try to identify them to find their level of adaption to the complexity and therefore their degree of proximity to my own research.

Within the current theories of team dynamics, the different development models can be classified according to their approach.

1.   Role models.

    Models based on the personal characteristics of their members. See the models of Margerison-McCann (1990) and Meredith Belbin (1981), (1993).

2.   Phase Models.

    Profiles based on the sequential succession of different development stages. See the Drexler-Sibbet models (Drexler, Sibbet, & Forrester, 1988), Tuckman (1965), (1977), Bennis (Bennis & Shepard, 1956) and Schein (2004).

3.   Stage models.

    The group adopts different status. See the Bion model (Bion, 1991).

In a first and rapid analysis to know the impact that these authors have had on the academic and business world it is enough to see the amount of results that Google Academic[3] gives to them. I use this source as search engine for academic documents due to the relative unawareness that there is of some of these models, in the measure that means amplifying the possible origins or sources of the mentioned quotes.

---

[3] Google Academic allows searching specialized bibliography. It is possible to make searches for a large number of skills and sources like, for example, studies revised by specialists, thesis, books, summaries and articles from sources like academic editorials, professional associations, preliminary print deposits, universities, etc.

The models are chronologically organized and presented and not by number of quotes. That is, from the most current to the oldest, according to the original publication of the model. As an exception, the Schein model has not been included in the summary of quotes but it has been analyzed. This is because the Schein study theme is the organizational structure and not the teamwork therefore in some way the quotes will refer to the first theme, the true objective of his study, and not the one we are interested in.

Author	_Work and date of original publication_	_# quotes_
Margerison, C.- McCann, D.	Team management: practical new approaches, 1990	31
Drexler, A.B.- Sibbet, D.	The team performance model, 1988	19
Belbin, R.M.	Management Teams. Why they succeed or fail, 1981	699
	Team Roles at Work, 1993	428
Tuckman, B.W.	Developmental sequences in small groups, 1965	1.219
	Stages of small group development revisited, 1977	551
Bion W. R.	Experiences in Groups, 1961	608
Bennis W.G.	A Theory of Group Development, 1956	355

Table 2-1: Group development models

The Tuckman model clearly is that which has had more repercussion in the academic world and by extension in the business, although as we see, nevertheless, it is one of the oldest. It will be necessary therefore to give it special attention and meticulously analyze it.

The model I introduce below differs from all the previous ones above all in contemplating the dimension of complexity. The proposed model is intimately linked to the evolution moment of the group in terms of desirable behaviour in front of external situations with growing complexity. In this sense it could seem that it is similar to the phase models if it were not for the existing correlation between the three levels of my model. This implies that they are dependent and although there is a certain focus of attention on each one of them, the three begin at the same time and should considered as a whole.

2.2   The Tuckman model (1965)

2.2.1   Description of model

Without doubt, the model that Bruce Wayne Tuckman (1965) published in an article about the stages of team developments[4] is a reference for the majority of studiers. Based on his systematic revision of empirical studies, he identified four fundamental phases, that even with some limitations, adequately resumed the mentioned process. At all times the studies are related with the interpersonal field and with that of the task, describing the phases as:

Forming. From the development viewpoint of the team, the author defines the first phase as *testing and dependence*. The members discover which behaviours are accepted in the group based on the reactions of the therapist[5] or shaper. They find out, testing, which are the frontiers of the situation. From the development viewpoint of the activity towards the task, labelled as *orientation to task*. The members of the group will try to identify the task in terms of its most relevant parameters and in such a way that the group experience will use to complement it. The group should decide which type of information it will need and how it should obtain it.

Storming. The second phase in the development structure of the group is called *intragroup conflict*. The members of the group become hostile with each other or towards the shaper or the therapist as an expression of their individuality and resistance to forming the group. The lack of unity is the most outstanding characteristic of this phase. From the task viewpoint this is labelled as *emotional response to task demands*. The group has an emotional answer to the task demands and disagrees about the orientation to cover such demands.

Norming. This third phase is called *development of group cohesion*; the members accept themselves as a group as well as the different idiosyncrasies of its members.

The desire of maintain and perpetuating the group appears and regulations are established to assure the existence of the group. Harmony acquires maximum importance and conflicts are avoided to assure it. Form the task point of view, this phase is defined as *open exchange of relevant interpretations*. It takes the shape of a discussion between one's self and the other members of the group.

---

[4] This article was re-printed in Group Facilitation: A Research and Applications Journal n° 3, 2001 and is available as a Word document at:
http://dennislearningcenter.osu.edu/references/GROUP%20DEV%20ARTICLE.doc (consulted in June 2009).

[5] Tuckman reviewed studies from the therapeutic practice environment, from training to natural groups and laboratory groups. In the first, the objective was to help the individuals with their personal problems; in the second, the objective was training; the third existed to carry out some social or professional function and the last were groups especially convened to study a specific phenomenon.

Performing. The fourth development phase of the group is called *functional role relatedness*. The group has become established as an entity in the previous phase and can now become an instrument for resolving problems. The relationship among the members is now consolidated and now can accept a role that improves the activities of the group toward the task. Form the task point of view this phase is called *emergence of solutions*. Here we can see constructive attempts to contribute to success of the task.

There is an essential correspondence in all the phases between the group structure and the task field. In both scopes emphasis falls on the constructive action and both go together is such a way that all the energy previously invested in the relational structure later reverts on resolving the task.

Tuckman himself, nevertheless, warns that this classification is conceptual and suggested by analyzed studies, in such a way that it is subject to posterior confirmations. He expressly cites limitations form literature, in the measure in that this cannot be considered as completely representative of the development of small groups. He admits that an overrepresentation of the therapeutic groups and the T-groups was seen in detriment of the natural and laboratory groups.

He also suggests the necessity of working in a more rigorously methodological way, beyond unique observations, with the aim of systematically manipulating the independent variables.

Stage	Group Structure	Task Activity
Forming	tests dependence definition of group limits	orientation to the task identification of relevant information definition of the way of obtaining the information
Storming	conflict hostility resistance to forming the group. disunion	emotional answer to the task demands discrepancies about the direction to be taken
Norming	common acceptance appearance of rules desire to perpetuate the group harmony	open discussion
Performing	definition of functional role	emergence of solutions

Table 2-2: The Tuckman model

Years later, together with Mary Ann Conover Jensen, he revised his later studies trying to verify his hypothesis, to which he finally added a fifth phase (Tuckman & Jensen, 1977).

The analyzed studies (except one) were not trying to prove any previous theoretical model but rather reflecting empirical research. Some of them coincided with the phases of the Tuckman model while others fusioned some of them, added other new ones or eliminated some. Once again they were slowed down by the research methodology used in spite of which it seemed reasonable to later add a final phase that insistently was documented in many of them. This phase referred to the termination of the group and to the uneasiness produce by its disappearance due to previously having developed strong interpersonal feelings. He called this phase **Adjourning**. Once again he warns about the limitations of adding and the necessity of posterior confirmations.

There are clear parallelisms between the phases defined by Tuckman and some of the observations made in Synergy that although I later catalogue them differently it is important to mention them.

Tuckman model	Synergy observations
Forming	At the very beginning of the session, the dependence on the shaper is absolute given that the group lacks the necessary knowledge to operate. By means of questions and experimenting, they will find out the necessary knowledge to start and obtain minimum results.
Storming	The intragroup conflict does not happen in Synergy in a generalized way or as a phase of individual expression. Right to the contrary, the groups that identify the interdependence of their situation easily accept exploring ways of collaboration. Although it is also true that when part of the group advances this way and another part refuses, in an effort to maintain their individuality, conflicts of will and interest appear.
Norming	The parallelism between the Tuckman phases of regulation in the development process of the cohesion is absolutely clear in Synergy. The participants create rules to identify themselves as a group. The rules and the cohesion are a consequence that emerges from the necessity of uniting efforts. Achieving a common project causes the group to cohesion.
Performing	At the end of the evolving process of the group and when it feels cohesioned, it is normal to see a common search for solutions. The participants spontaneously interchange information; they commonly warn of risks and opportunities and dynamically coordinate themselves.

Table 2-3: Similarities with the Tuckman model

2.2.2   Posterior developments to the Tuckman model

Assessment models have been developed on the basis of the Tuckman model that pretend to infer on the development of the groups, fundamentally with the goal of making them sequentially evolve to the last phase. Such models enrich the analysis of each one of the phases incorporating aspects that are not contemplated in the original model. The same way they design an optimal way of acting to be carried out both by the group members as by its leaders, according to the phase of the group. Therefore they assume the model in all its consequences, including its limitations, and on occasions obviating that the initial intention of Tuckman was that of helping comprehension of the development of small groups through the proposed classification, warning of the necessity of a posterior confirmation by means of studies to that effect.

2.2.3   Criticism of the model

Stephen Robbins (1999) analyzes the limitations of the model so that we could catalogue them in the following manner:

> **This is a sequential model.** Many interpreters of the model with five phases have assumed that the group becomes more efficient as it progresses through the first four phases. Although this general premise could be true, what causes a group to become efficient is more complex than what this model admits. In certain conditions, high levels of conflict lead to high performance of the group. Thus we could expect to find situations where the groups of the II phase overtake those in phases III or IV.

> **The categorization of the phases is diffuse.** Similarly, the groups do not always proceed with clarity from one phase to the next. Sometimes, in fact, several phases coexist at the same time, like when the groups are in the storm or in the performance at the same time.

> **It is a lineal model.** The groups, even occasionally, return to the previous phases. Therefore even the most active defenders of this model do not assume that all the groups follow the process of the five phases with precision or that the IV phase is always the preferred one.

> **It is a decontextualized model.** Another problem with the model of the five phases, in terms of understanding the behaviour related with the group, is that it ignores the organizational context. The contexts supply rules, task definitions, information and necessary resources to develop group task. They do not need to develop, planning, assigning roles, determining and distributing resources, resolving conflicts, or establishing rules in the way that the model of five phases predicts.

Lastly, it would be ideal to question the names, which Tuckman used for each one of the phases. Without taking merit away from his success, after all they have survived up to our days; we could attribute to him a certain reductive effect. When comparing it with his definitions of the phases we see that they are centred on concrete aspects, leaving to one side other possible aspects to be considered in each one of them.

Nevertheless it is only right to adequately evaluate the work carried out by Tuckman and the enormous qualitative jump made to understand the work teams.

CHAPTER 3

THE SIMULATION

3.1 The course

The teamwork course for managers consists in an action of two complete days that by means of real time group dynamics and using a game interface in a recreational manner, it transports the groups to an environment of growing complexity. The groups act following the processes of making decisions and the integrated organizational guidelines which leads them to a situation of incompetence in the new environment to which they should respond. The dynamics provoke a crisis, which forces them to reconsider their way of working and understand the cause of their difficulties and of their poor answer.

The work training course as a team is vehicularized by means of a simulator called Synergy. Synergy is a simulator where the participants in a cyclic way first receive instructions about the use of the simulator, prepare the game cycle in question, play, obtain reports and finally analyze together with the teacher, the results, the dynamics, the academic references and their extrapolation to real life.

The direct observation model used is also especially useful for the objective of the present work inasmuch as it does not imply any hassle, obstruction, or interruption of any type. The participants can spontaneously operate without feeling observed or having to interrupt their relationship processes. This means that the situation is equivalent to a real environment of decision making by the management team.

3.2 Using simulators in training

Since when Peter Senge wrote "The Fifth Discipline" (Senge, 1990) and helped the diffusion of the system concept, its application to social systems has been more and more clear and evident. In a world of growing complexity, in constant change and more and more interrelated, a partial, simple and single disciplined approximation to try understanding and handling, would be impossible. On his part, Jay Forrester of the MIT, in 1961 already introduced the dynamics concepts of systems applied to mediation (Forrester, 1961). Computer tools developed since then facilitate the creation of these causal models.

The new training disciplines based on Gaming/Simulation, are capable of dramatically using the development of explanatory models by means of Systems Dynamics, based on Systems Thinking of social and economic reality, using all the possibilities of new technologies to develop Business Simulators, capable of being used in higher training dynamics, both at universities as well as in organizations. The result is training acquired through experience in life that uniting cognition and emotion allows the participant to understand and integrate complex and dynamic contexts.

Experiential learning that allows gaming/simulation favours the change of necessary mental schemes for learning and organizational evolution.

3.3   Simulation & Gaming as research methodology

We define the simulation as a "partial representation of reality, that chooses crucial characteristics from a real situation and makes a replica of them within an environment essentially free from risk allowing the participants to develop their strategies to resolve a determined challenge" (Saunders & Powell, 1998).

We define play/simulation as "an activity that works, entirely or partially, on the basis of the players' decisions. The simulation is an operative model that has the abstraction and the representation of a larger system" (Tsuchiya & Tsuchiya, 1999).

Therefore we distinguish between the simulation as a representation exercise and the play/simulation as a human relational activity that takes the mentioned simulation as an instrument. The subtle difference is of special relevance when the play/simulations create a new shared mental model.

3.4   Results

The method that was used is based on the observation of behaviours of the company directors that formed the sample. These, faced with the resolution of the situation proposed in the course, repeated in more or less measure a series of behaviours that were structured and systematically recompiled to be analyzed.

As the course evolved around a business simulator that measures results obtained by the groups, later it was possible to relate the results with the behaviours of each group.

The results obtained after different statistical treatments indicate that effectively teamwork in high complexity situation is significantly related to the results. The data also indicates the nonexistence of phases, understood as temporary sequences.

CHAPTER 4

KNOWLEDGE

4.1   Observation variables

The first activity of the groups is always the acquisition of sufficient knowledge as to allow them to minimally handle the proposed environment. In this sense the observations I make of the participants have two orientations, one toward obtaining results and the other toward building relations.

1) The first orientation of their activities is towards results. It consists in obtaining data by means of requesting more information and the clarification of that already received; in making action decisions and in controlling results. I call this variable Proactivity of results.

2) The second is toward relations. It consists in interest in the task of others, the interchange of information and joint analysis and the intent of building relations and sharing experiences. I call this variable Proactivity to relations.

The result of this proactive attitude in an environment of uncertainty like that proposed at the beginning of the simulation is the acquisition of knowledge. Everything occurs in an individual scope where we understand the individual not as a person but rather as an agent with independent capacity to take decisions. Extrapolating this to reality an agent could be a person, a department, an area of the organization, etc., as long as it acts as a sole agent making decisions in a larger system. In fact in the simulation we understand the individual to be the subdivision of the group. If the group is the twelve participants, the subdivision is the three that form a department and in the group there are four.

4.2   Experiential learning

Kurt Zadek Lewin (September 99, 1890 – February 12, 1947), considered as the father of organizational development for his contribution from the Research Centre for Group Dynamics in the Massachusetts Institute of Technology, in Field Theory in Social Sciences where he describes the learning cycle in a four state cycle. From concrete experience observations are obtained that by means of reflection and analysis they allow conceptualization and whose conclusions and hypothesis are compared in a new experience that modifies the behaviour of the actor, reinitiating the cycle.

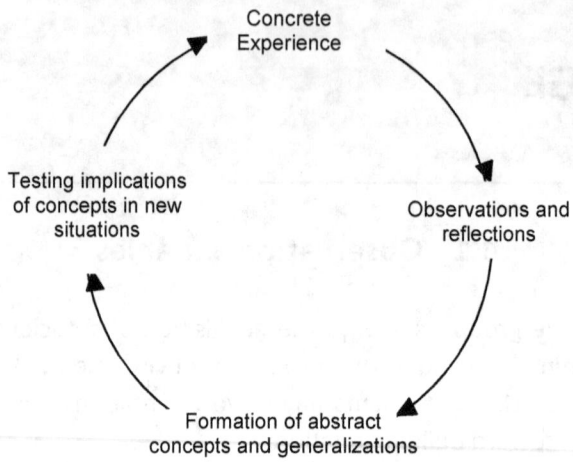

Illustration 4-1: Kurt Lewin experiential learning cycle

4.3 Learning from mistakes

On 20 August 2008 one of the worst air accidents in Spain occurred in Madrid. 154 people died. The draft of the report from the Spanish Civil Aviation Accident and Incident Research Commission (CIAIAC, Spanish initials) about the accident indicated that the MD-82 did not have the flaps out (the aileron that provide support to the airplane during take-off) and that the warning system did not warn the pilot of this abnormality which would have avoided the fatal accident. A similar fault happened in the accident of another MD-82 in Detroit in 1987. The Take-Off Warning System (TOWS) did not work. In addition, 154 people died in this accident. As the draft from the Accident Research Commission indicates, the manufacturer of the aircraft McDonnell-Douglas (now Boeing) then "recommended" that the companies should always check this safety system that warns of abnormalities during take-off before each flight. However, Spanair only specifies in its protocols that the check should be made before the first flight of the day or when both pilots are changed. The Spanair director of operations, justified this saying "The recommendation was over 20 years ago. Spanair did not exist and we do not have any knowledge of having received that recommendation. It was from 1987, Spanair started in 1988". The CIAIAC has asked the EU and USA that this revision before take-off is obligatory. On 5 June 2007, an MD-83 of the Austrian company Mapjet was near to crashing in Lanzarote due to similar causes[6]. How could this happen, you may ask, having there been previous accidents and failures of such magnitude?

One of the best sources of learning in complex environments are one's own mistakes, the second best is the mistakes of others. During the whole learning process that is given in the seminar, those groups that are capable of identifying the origin of errors and learning from them in experience, are those that more rapidly develop the training. In organizations learning from mistakes becomes an essential part that should not be covered-up or avoided (Sitkin, 1995). Much too frequently small errors are obviated due to fear of reprisals or reproach from organizational supervisors. Sitkin explained how in successful organizations errors create a risk recognition and motivation for change. Other times the contrary could happen, that the key to learning is precisely the capacity of unlearning policies or practices that having been valid in the past, have become obsolete due to changes in the environment.

Very frequently it is seen how in the training seminar, groups that were successful in the last but one cycle of the game, failed in achieving the objectives of the last cycle due to considering that change was not necessary. In addition, to the contrary, the mistakes made stimulated the group to look for new solutions learning from them. Sitkin indicates that not all faults allow learning, only those so-called intelligent ones and that comply with the following characteristics:

1. They are the result of deliberately planned actions.
2. They have uncertain results.
3. They are of a modest scale, small.
4. They are executed and have rapid answers, not delaying in time.
5. They have place in sufficiently familiar environments as to allow effective learning.

Every organization with sufficient memory will be capable of avoiding repetition of those faults already committed. To the contrary, those organizations incapable of acquiring and distributing knowledge will be compelled to repeating past experiences. Occasionally, organizations release key employees or those with much experience, without considering the adequate training for the replacement or the mechanisms for recuperation of that knowledge that undoubtedly will be lost with their separation from the company.

---

[6] Source: El País newspaper library.

4.4 Proactivity

Proactivity to relations and proactivity to results are the variables of the individual scope of the model we analyze here. Proactivity is one of those words that everyone knows, identifies and uses but are not really in the dictionary[7]. On the other hand we can find the adjective proactive or the adverb proactively. Defined as "create or control a situation instead of only answering to it" or "acting to provoke changes and not only reacting to the change when this happens" the concept is clearly related to anticipation.

In spite of there not being a sole definition or theory or a standard measure of the construct we could talk of proactive behaviour as the taking of initiatives for improving current circumstances of for the creation of new ones (Crant, 2000). Therefore it refers to challenging the status quo more than the passive adaptation to current conditions. Proactive behaviour is due to both personal differences as to contextual factors. Bateman y Crant (cited by Crant, 2000) introduces the proactive disposition as a construct that identifies differences between persons in the measures that these act to influence their environment.

A prototype proactive personality would be that which is not limited by forces of the moment and introduces changes in the environment. Proactive persons identify opportunities and act according to them; they show initiative, take action and persevere until significant changes happen. In studies carried out with the Bateman and Crant proactive personality scale (PPS) relations are demonstrated with individual work results, with the evolution of professional careers, with leadership, with organizational innovation, with team results and with entrepreneur capacity.

From an environment point of view, people learn from what they see and react accordingly. Regarding this we define socialization in organizations and work teams as "a process of common adjustment that produces changes in time between a person and the group" (Moreland & Levine, 2006). The interpretation of the context and the intentions of the socializing agents affect the answer and levels of activity.

A study over 102 new incorporations in 96 firms supports this approach (Jones cited by Crant, 2000). Organizational tactics like formal collective programs oriented to the interchange of experiences facilitate the orientation towards more proactive roles. Feedback is another valuable resource at the time of facilitating proactive behaviour in the measure that helps achieving objectives. Management support, culture or regulations will also be contextual factors that can favour it.

---

[7] Not in the Diccionario de la Real Academia Española, but it is in the Oxford English Dictionary or in the Cambridge English Dictionary.

18

CHAPTER 5

COHESION

5.1   Observation variables

After the acquisition of basic knowledge to function, the activity that most clearly reflects the group is the relationship between its members. This relationship, that leads to a high level of cohesion, higher in groups with better results, goes through the process of integration for which common confidence is vital.

1) The integration of the group is the first variable of the cohesion process. It reflects cooperation behaviours, a complete system of general rules to establish the team limits that conceptually are acquiring their own meaning and the implication of its members.

2) Generation of confidence is the second variable. It is the consequence of equality and generosity. The group shares loads and benefits in equality and it assures that no member of the incipient team will obtain benefit at others expense. Generosity assures that the first decision of the participants will be beneficial for the group. Whenever it is for individual benefit it provokes rejection and impedes consolidation of relations.

The result of integration and generosity will be a consolidated team, conscious of itself and with the capacity to keep advancing. To the contrary, those groups that are not consolidated are not able to renounce to individualist positions and do not find therefore other ways than mere technical improvements.

5.2   Definition of cohesion

Cohesion has always been considered as one of the most important variables in all group analysis. Its definition normally is in connection with the union strength of a group. One of the earliest definitions in this sense was that of Festinger who defined it as the whole scope of forces that act over the members to remain in the group (Festinger, Schacter, & Back, 1950). A more up-to-date definition was given by the professor of the University of Western Ontario, Albert V. Carron who defines cohesion as "a dynamic process that reflects the tendency of a group to unite and remain united in the achievement of its instrumental objectives and/or the satisfaction of the affective necessities of its members" (Carron, Brawley, & Widmeyer, 1998).

Cohesion has the effect of making the group members feel well through the feeling of internal unity and facilitating change and collaborative actions. A cohesioned group tends to emotionally unite its members in connection with a task and with themselves, assuring better group stability and improving corporative diversity (Lakin, 1972).

5.3 Integration process

If there is anything clear in the courses it is the integration process they follow. At the beginning there is hardly any contact and when it happens, it is merely as an exploration. Until a minimum level of technical knowledge is reached, contacts do not have a defined objective. It is when the group senses what they have in hand they start to relate with each other with common interests. The first they do is to define collaboration spaces in those more evident aspects where they all win. This point is very satisfactory because it makes them think that they are collaborating but it is very short-lived because it has a low potential for development.

The game continues and they should look for other alternatives that open new ways of collaboration. At that moment they start to explore that, which without individual harm does benefit others, that is to say it benefits some and does not harm anyone. In this point we see the dilemma of correspondence. How to assure a return on investment? How to measure individual contributions so that in that negotiating process, value is equally shared? Two interesting phenomenon appear now, the necessity of equality and the creation of regulations. At this level, the group seems to confirm the theory of equity according to which the individuals compare their individual contributions and the benefits they receive with those of the others and respond by eliminating inequalities (Adams, 1965).

The group considers that to be able to continue cooperating and as the options of individual benefit are clear, while those of common benefit are not, the benefit obtained should be shared. Likewise the cost or harm of collaboration should be shared. If this was not the case, an individual subgroup could think that there is no point in collaborating as the load would be higher than the cost and that would cause it the loss of opportunities to achieve its individual objective. To assure equality the participants create a whole series of regulations that assure an equal share out. That regulatory process has a key effect by limiting action in such a way that allows identifying belonging to the group. Whoever does not follow the rules is not considered as part of the group and to the contrary of those that do, on occasions in spite of the result, it is considered the price to be paid for cohesion. It is the emotional border between group and team.

The level reached is satisfactory by it is still not optimal. Clearly a management mechanism based on equality has the result of equal sharing but not the maximization of results. One of the systems thinking principles becomes patent that says the maximization of the parts does not necessarily implicate maximization of the whole. Much to the contrary, by detracting resources from the system to equalize results, the performance levels required by the game are still not achieved. The team should continue to search. Here is where all that which many times is intuitively related to teamwork and that has to do with generosity, with altruism and with faith more that calculations, comes into play.

The group starts to take decisions thinking of common benefit and understanding this concept no as the sum of all but as a new differentiated entity. Now it is not a matter of doing that, which benefits everyone, or even negotiating and obtaining benefits in exchange for something, it is a matter of doing that, which benefits the whole group, trusting in that the reciprocity will arrive and that the effort will give its fruits. A maximum level of implication is obtained at this moment. The participants have fusioned, integrated in something new, a team.

During the process of integration I identify some of the themes that Edgar Schein proposes as part of the internal integration process (Schein, 2004).

Edgar Schein Internal Integration Issues	Synergy observations
Creation of a common language	The group identifies the terminology capable of explaining concepts handled in the simulator creating specific concepts.
Definition of group limits and criterion of inclusion and exclusion.	The group clearly establishes the decisions that will identify who work in cooperation or individually.
Power and status distribution	The members relate in accord to clear identifications of power and leadership.
Development of regulations.	Fully defined, the group identifies what should be done, what is advisable do and what should not be done.
Definition of compensations and punishments	When any of these regulations is infringed the group aggressively reacts against who does not respect it.
Explanation of that unexplainable.	That which escapes the knowledge that the group has accumulated until now is placed at the front as something necessary at that moment and the existence of which will be clarified further on.

Table 5-1: Group integration matters according to Schein

5.4 Definition of trust

The second variable to appear at cohesion level is trust. Historically trust has been the object of many studies that fundamentally relate it with leadership but also with positive attitudes of work, organizational justice, psychological contract, effective communication, organizational relations, conflict management, etc. The role of trust in a long term committed relationship is also considered as crucial to establish and maintain a cooperative balance.

From all the different definitions of trust in organizational theory we could use here as a more adequate definition, "the expectation of positive behaviour that recognizes and protects the interests of other persons, in such a way that the probability of cooperation increases and expands the final benefits within a common effort or economic interchange" (Hosmer, 1995).

5.5 The importance of equality

I have already spoken of the importance of equality when I referred to integration. There comes a time when it becomes patent that to evolve in integration, generate more cohesion, become conscious of the group, and advance in collaboration, etc., it is necessary to go through a phase of equality. In addition, I refer to it as a phase because it clearly means an evolutionary moment that did not exist before and should be overcome later. During this phase of equality the group, through some clearly defined rules, measures-up the members, facing them with enforced situations. Alternatively, one is with the group, even at the cost of the individual, or one is against it.

If the majority of the group opts to become consolidated as a team and someone remains in the margin, the team has possibilities of evolving, but not without any emotional friction. If the majority stays on the margin, the evolution of the group fails and it returns to individualist positions and not cooperative ones. If the majority advances it is when some members self-excludes himself by making individualist decisions, depending on the importance of the decision, of the moment and the impact it has had, it could abort the global evolution or simply provoke a violent exclusion reaction. All that from a purely emotional point of view without paying attention to the reasons, legitimate or not for such self-exclusion decisions.

This is an important reflection because it indicates to us that one cannot abort the integration process until the group has generated sufficient trust so that these apparently individualist decisions are understood, are contextualized, or even mange to improve, by variation, the process of group decision making. Therefore it will be a capacity of capital importance for the leading coordinator, to maintain a global and dynamic perspective that allows him to identify the evolutionary moment of the group.

With he could know if he should strengthen the overcoming of the phase or to the contrary maintain it in spite of the cost of achieving the necessary degree of cohesion.

Having said this latter it is also necessary to also underline that at the beginning it is difficult for the group to pass through the equality phase as this strengthens the cohesion. When the level of trust is considered to be sound enough, it will be the moment to introduce the reconsideration of processes and decisions that have been established as adequate.

CHAPTER 6

SELF-COORDINATION

6.1   Observation variables

When the groups become a team and has unit conscience, the feeling of cohesion allows them to commonly approach the solutions but their implementation needs defining an operational set-up. In a constantly changing complex situation like that proposed by the simulator it would not be possible to establish centralized coordination mechanisms so the team needs criterion more than instructions.   The equal relationship and criterion are the observation variables in this process.

1) The equal relationship is the first variable of self-coordination.   It is the consequence of common consideration and respect. It means the valuation and acceptance of different positions, organized non-violent discussion, construction instead of imposition, conviction more than submission.

2) The criterion of action is the second variable.   It is the consequence of the definition of a criterion, of its unification and of the establishment of another alternative.   It implies an identification and evaluation process to fix and unify a common criterion of action that nevertheless should have an alternative available in the case of being inadequate.

6.2   Equal relationship

Communication is an essential element in systems. Communication in symmetry[8], on equal terms, is a fundamental element of collaboration. Common respect and consideration are two easily perceivable factors and whose emotional impact is a key to motivate the corporate pass.

The Group Emotional Intelligence uses communication of appreciation, consideration and respect as affective orientation. Through that, the members of the group communicate that their group values the presence and contribution of each one of its

---

[8]Communication in symmetry (equality) is especially useful in the common development and analysis processes, which does not mean that it can coexist with communication in complementarity (inequality) when it means transferring views or objectives. Communication in symmetry is expressed from motivation while communication in complementarity is from demand.

members. In a study made in 67 work teams, Druskat and Wolff found that an affective orientation contributed to the effectiveness and increased the sensation of security, cohesion and satisfaction of the members who in turn facilitated carrying out the tasks (Druskat & Wolff, 2005).

6.3   Criterion of action

Face to face with adequate self-coordination of the team, it will be necessary to define and unify a criterion of action. Beyond that we should identify a contingency plan as an alternative criterion, because in complexity any plan, although necessary, is only initially admitted as only one of the possibly valid options. Adequate criterion therefore will be the one that complements the planning with feedback control, flexibility and capacity for reaction.

The definition of the criterion of action is the main element in making decisions. Therefore we can identify the making of decisions as the manifestation of this criterion. In complexity the capacity for establishing a criterion and making decisions is not easy due to the rationality of individuals is bounded by the information they have, the cognitive limitations of their minds, and the finite quantity of time they have to take decisions (Simon, 1997). Simon faces this bounded rationality with the objective rationality of an economic man taking the following three phases:

1. Analysis of the options are possible alternatives
2. Prevision and consideration of the consequences derived from each option
3. Establishment of system of values as criterion of selection.

This process is faced with at least three limitations:

1. Rationality requires full knowledge and anticipation the consequences of each option.
2. Values subject to the consequences, as these occur in the future, can only be anticipated in an imperfect manner.
3. Rationality requires being able to choose among all the possible behaviours and only a few of them can be anticipated.

For that reason and for the fact that a human being can only know a fraction of the knowledge that surrounds an action, a strictly rational decision is not possible. Alternatively, the administrator (in terms of Simon) should satisfy more than maximize without examining all the possible alternative behaviours and assuming that those are in fact "all" the alternatives.

CHAPTER 7

THE COOPLEXITY MODEL

7.1 Introduction

As a consequence of the observation of behaviour of the different management teams I identified three fundamental processes in their action.

The first was oriented to the acquisition of knowledge through learning. Nevertheless this is not independent of the environment, not even isolated from the other members. Learning is a circular gestation process and comparing hypothesis that include relations with others. Therefore experimentation is a key in the building of knowledge. The observation variable were as follows

PROCESS	VARIABLES	OBSERVATIONS
Knowledge acquisition	Proactivity oriented to results	Obtaining data Making action decisions Control of objective
	Proactivity oriented to relations	Interaction Interchange Relation

The second process is oriented to the group cohesion. Integration of the group and generation of trust is produced around the attempt of the group to achieve a common objective. At this evolutionary moment, the existence of a common project becomes the motive for cohesion.

PROCESS	VARIABLES	OBSERVATIONS
Integration and cohesion of the group	Group integration	Cooperation Normalization Implication
	Trust generation	Equality Generosity

In the third process, collaboration is shown at its highest point and coordination is the key to efficient performance. Shared leadership is essentially the result of emergence at this level. The team reaches here functioning in a totally interdependent manner as a consequence of the action initiatives that it has been taking when exploring ways of collaboration and possible joint actions. With a higher number of interconnections, this shared leadership appears more easily, and with that, the capacity of the team to self-coordinate.

PROCESS	VARIABLES	OBSERVATIONS
Self-coordination	Equal relationship	Common consideration Respect
	Criterion of action	Definition of criterion Unification of criterion Alternative criterion

Around these fundamental processes and these observation variables I propose the Cooplexity model of collaboration that would become a dynamic, evolving, cooperative and collaborative model this way, in situations of uncertainty and complexity.

7.2 The collaboration model

7.2.1 Scopes of the model: individual, group and team

In that evolutionary process and as complexity increases each active subject is different. At the beginning I identify individuals, that later form a group that finally becomes team conscious.

Initially they are **individuals** that experiment, investigate, compare and learn. By individuals I do not only mean an individual person but rather a unit of independent decision. In this sense the concept of individual scope would be related to agents that in reality could be departments, areas, factories, affiliates, companies or any other group independent of its size.

Nest, these agents, that in the simulator are subgroups of three persons, form a **group**. This new main character differs from the previous one in that it groups several agents and adds relations between them. In turn the group continues exploring, searching for solutions, investigating, but also it does that by trying to find common points of support, help and complementarily mechanisms.

Finally the **team** appears if the group has become consolidated and cohesioned. The fundamental difference is that they become conscious of themselves as a new entity. They have different characteristics from when they were a group in the sense that their relations become interrelations, they have a clear interdependence, they are conscious of how their decisions have a common affect, they consider each other and above all they have a common objective that should be built by the entire team. Their decisions are the result of a balance between individual and common positions and interests. In addition, all that occurs without friction, in a natural and spontaneous manner and more like the result of an agreement than of a negotiation.

7.2.2   Levels in Synergy

When identifying the main processes, which cause the evolution of the team and circumscribing them to individual, group and team scopes, we are implicitly recognizing three clearly differentiated levels.

That way in the individual scope, the process for acquiring knowledge as a fundamental activity of the group in the first states, means a previous level of development. During a first moment of uncertainty, the experimentation and acquisition of knowledge, both of functions and of relations, becomes the level differential function.

After having acquired knowledge the following level is that of the group cohesion process. In this group scope we see the first relations of approximation that lead to the integration process and are founded on the generation of trust.

Having passed the second level, the third, related to self-coordination will centre all the group activity on reaching the objectives based on their capacity of self-organization. Autonomy, common criterion of action, decentralized decision making process and distributed knowledge, all coincide with a cohesioned team, conscious of itself and with the necessary experience and knowledge to facilitate the emergence of leaderships and of distributed initiatives that would lead to self-coordination.

7.2.3   Synergy catalyzers

There was always a catalyzer in the three identified levels capable of provoking or causing their evolution.

The first level, identified as individual scope, is fundamentally oriented to the acquisition of knowledge. In a known environment someone or something is capable of transferring knowledge. Books, manuals, technical magazines, symposiums, conferences, courses, databases, protocols, programs. There are a multitude of mechanisms for transferring knowledge. In the real world even that knowledge can be obtained directly by hiring experts, collaborations and partnerships or even mergers or acquisitions.

In an unknown environment that learning is done by experimentation. Nevertheless this is not independent of the environment, not even isolated from the other members. Here training is a circular gestation process and comparing hypothesis that includes relations with others.

An if experimenting to learn is the leitmotiv of the firs level, **proactive exploration** both oriented to results as to relations leads to experimentation and with that learning, especially in situations of uncertainty.

The second level that identified as group scope occurs with group cohesion. Integration of the group and the generation of trust are produced around the attempt of the group to achieve a **common objective**. At this evolutionary moment, the existence of a common project becomes the motive for cohesion. The effort that the group makes to convert the project into common and to unite its interests, balancing their own and collective ones, is fundamental for team gestation.

Finally the **interconnections** are the self-coordination level catalyzer in the team scope. For self-coordination to exist the creation of the necessary conditions that allow individual initiative and the appearance of spontaneous leaderships are fundamental. In Self-coordination, the results depend largely on the capacity that the team has of managing complexity and of identifying opportunities and risks. Therefore, joint analysis, complementarity of view points, richness of approach due to diversity, individual spontaneous initiative and complementarity will be very important. Nevertheless co-leaderships are not something we can directly act on. We should go round them creating and managing the necessary conditions for them to appear. Those interconnections allow knowledge crossing by the agents, of their activity, of their interests, of their needs.

7.2.4   Communication in Synergy

Communication plays a fundamental role and has an impact over the whole group development process. Initially it is a key in proactivity oriented to relations. Next integration and cohesion are vitally important in the whole group cohesion process. Once again equal relationship is main character of self-coordination. Therefore it is not an independent or isolated characteristic; neither constitutes a phase or level by itself. Communication happens throughout the whole process, from start to finish becoming vitally important in the global evolution and being the second axis of the model.

The perspective of communication in this case has to be seen from constructivist and constructionist psychology viewpoint that knowledge is obtained through self experience.

Constructivism is oriented toward personality and educational psychology, and Constructionism toward social and political psychology. Both currents start from the same epistemological base,[9] given by the thesis that knowledge consists of a

---

[9] Theories can be studied and organized in accord with ontology, epistemology and axiology. Ontology places emphasis in what is being examined, which is its true nature. The answer generally speaking can have a realistic approach (objective), or nominalist (subjective) or constructionalist (real it is what we agree to be real). Epistemology refers to how the examination is done. It studies the foundations and methods of scientific knowledge. The purpose of epistemology is to distinguish authentic science from pseudoscience, in-depth research from superficial. Axiology in turn is the branch of philosophy that studies the nature of values and evaluatory judgements.

psychological and social reality builder process, and the consequence that human behaviour is not biased but determined by the mentioned process (Munné, 1999)[10].

Communication, taking into account what we have seen up to now, should be understood in the model to be decisive of the relations between the members and the one responsible of the evolution through the different individual, group, and team scopes.

7.2.5 Graphic representation of the Cooplexity model

Because of all seen up to now, I propose a theoretical collaboration model, which I call Cooplexity. The name refers to a Cooperation-Collaboration Model in Uncertainty and Complexity.

The three fundamental processes will be arranged in levels in Cooplexity. Each level means an objective to be reached for team development. In spite of how we have seen the three levels overlapping in time and therefore not forming independent phases, it is true that the differential activity of each level concentrates in a more significant way around sequential scopes. From a pedagogical point of view it is more graphic to draw the fundamental nucleus of the activity at each level as if it were an evolving process in time, starting from a common moment. This is how we represent that the construction of the three levels should be taken into consideration from the beginning and that all those group decisions help doing that, in spite of that the fundamental process of each level will require special attention when needed and in accord of the reached level of complexity.

This way each level will evolve regarding the two reference axis, one referring to the increase in complexity in time as a cause for the necessity of each level to evolve from the communication that makes transition between levels possible. Both axis, start from a minimal common point. This point represents the minimum quantity and necessary communication to apply to this model.

In each level, the observation variables will become factors, understanding these as causal elements of the level.

In the first level, the *Knowledge* one, the participants would develop an action oriented to exploitation and based on initiatives. The factors of the first level would be the "Proactivity to results" and the "Proactivity to relations".

As time goes by, the members of a group will get to know the keys to their environment and will have the necessary abilities for their still simple yet sufficient handling. Then they will enter the second level, that of *Cohesion*. Here, the "Group

---

[10] Accessible via portalpsicología.org http://www.portalpsicologia.org/servlet/File?idDocumento=2069 (consulted in June, 2009).

integration" and the "Trust generation" will be their corresponding causal factors. The common project and joint effort to achieve it will be the motive.

The group will start to perceive itself as a unit and will become self-conscious. Finally the group will feel they are a team, they will commonly consider each other and will communicate in symmetry with respect, giving way to the "Equal relationship" factor. The second level factor will refer to the definition and unification and at the best the identification of a contingency plan. It would be the "Criterion of action" factor. The equal relationship and the established criterion would allow *Self-coordination* thanks to the communication flow through the interconnections between members.

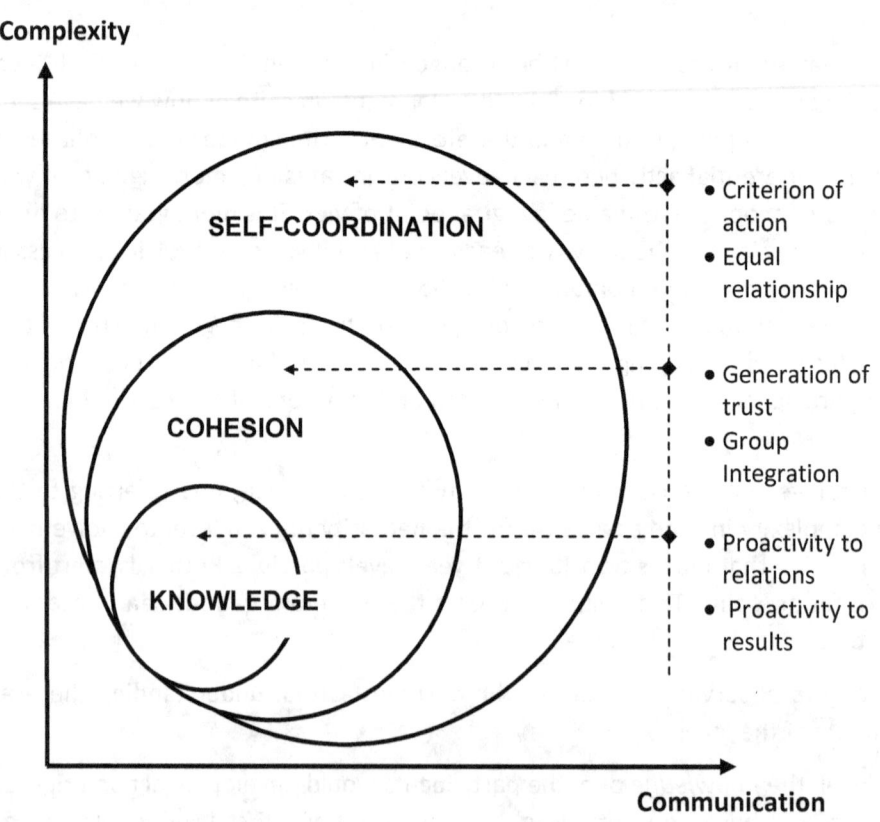

Illustration 7-1: Graphic representation of the Cooplexity model

7.2.6 "Teamworking Mix": EPIC

Besides finding a graphic way of explaining the model so that it easily understandable and identifiable, one of my wishes was to find a simple way of transmitting what I understand to be the keys to its success, an easy way of remembering them, of understanding their mechanisms and their application.

That is why I call "Teamworking Mix" the group of the four essential catalyzers of the model, identified by the acronym[11] **EPIC**:

Explore in the framework of common Project favouring Interconnections by means of Communication.

"Explore" freezes the fundamental action of acquiring knowledge in uncertainty, where the absence of information makes formation from already known or existing instruments less viable. It does not substitute but rather complements these other means (training, consulting, publications, etc.) but it emphasizes and concentrates the knowledge level factors, proactivity to results and to relations. Likewise it includes another aspect at this level, tolerance to failures and learning from mistakes, inherent to all experimentation and vital at the time of acquiring knowledge.

In the framework of a **"Common project"**, facing day-to-day activities, maintenance, repetition. A project challenges, concentrates attention and resources, stimulates and provokes. A common project is shared, helps team integration and trust generation. In terms of systems it is an attractor that catalyzes cohesion.

Favouring **"Interconnections"**, points of encounter, interchanges, interrelations, interdependencies. All that which allows a team with knowledge and cohesion to self-coordinate themselves in a spontaneous, natural and voluntary way. A team whose agents are interconnected has the necessary links for information to flow. Information added to the commitment to cohesion favours flexibility and adaptation, reaction to possible risks and taking advantage of opportunities.

By means of **"Communication"** understood as a social interaction instrument, as a mechanism not only for interchange but also as a building process. The agents when they communicate commonly affect each other giving way to new realities built as a consequence of those interactions. Communication from this perspective affects behaviour and this in turn is a means of communication.

---

[11] An acronym is a type of initials that are pronounced as a word, for example: u(nidentified) f(lying) o(bject). It is more useful for my purpose in this case because it does oblige forcing the name of each catalyser to make them coincide and to the contrary, it allows better identification of the final message.

7.3   Summary

Because of all seen up to now, I propose a theoretical team-work model, which I call Cooplexity: a Cooperation-Collaboration Model in Uncertainty and Complexity.

SCOPE	LEVELS	CATALYZERS	FACTORS	ACTIVITIES
Individual	*Knowledge*	Exploration	Proactivity oriented to results	Capture of data Taking action decisions Control of objective
			Proactivity oriented to relations	Interaction Interchange Relation
Group	*Cohesion*	Common project	Group integration	Cooperation Normalization Implication
			Trust generation	Equality Generosity
Team	*Self-coordination*	Interconnections	Equal relationship	Common consideration Respect
			Criterion of action	Definition of criterion Unification of criterion Alternative criterion

The acronym I propose so as to easily remember the keys of the model is **EPIC:** *Explore in the framework of common **P**roject favouring **I**nterconnections by means of **C**ommunication.*

CHAPTER 8

TEAM LEADERSHIP

8.1 The team leadership roles

An obligatory question when trying to carry out what was seen in the model is how the leader acts to try and achieve the results. In this case it is a trick question as it is precisely one of the things the model teaches is that there is not a leader in the traditional sense of the word but rather a series of them acting in a parallel, overlapped and spontaneous manner. This does not help a lot if we consider that in organizations there is usually only one person that agglutinates the responsibility of one function. The answer once again comes from the observation of how the participants act.

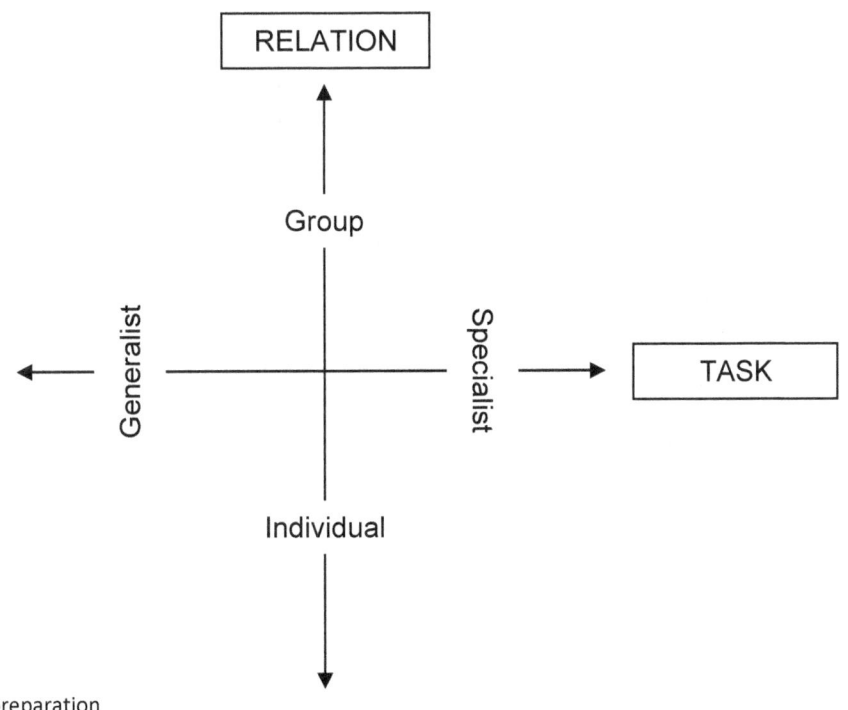

Source: Own preparation

Firstly we will consider a traditional dichotomy in the dimensional divisions of management like orientation to task and to relation. We can view it from a dynamic point of view where the relation can evolve from individual to collective and the task from general to special. The axis we would obtain that way would be as follows.

Now we place these axes in the context of the model, this is, referring to the levels of interrelation and interdependence that lead us to a situation of complexity.

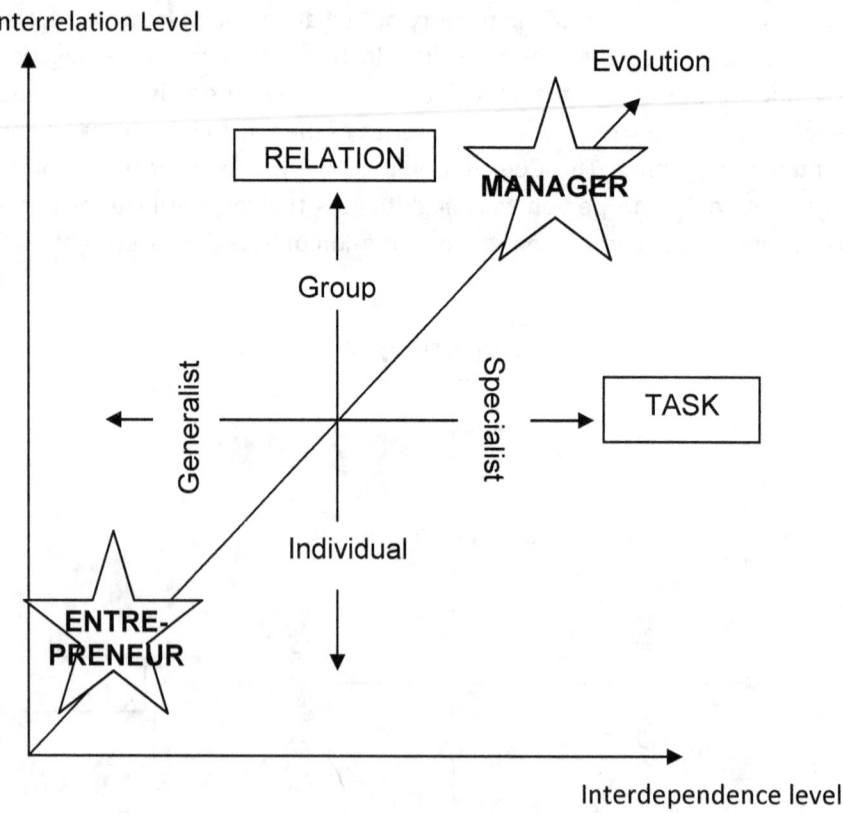

Source: Own preparation

Two extreme and opposed leadership manifestations appear, that one based on personal capacities, on intuition, on taking risks, on the capacity of influence and persuasion on personal charm, etc. that we can identify with the entrepreneur. At the other extreme we find the managing director of teams, wary to risks, respectful of rules, more professional, stable, secure and predictable.

The first would be capable of breaking schemes, creating, acting adequately in uncertainty and would be attracted by experimentation, for discovery. However he would be bored with organization when it is mature, complex, with levels of detail that he no longer controls. The second, to the contrary, would be attracted by size, complexity, interrelations. More political and capable with relations he coordinates more than does, connects more than he thinks.

Recent studies have identified the differences between both profiles around bias and heuristics (inquiry and discovery). The entrepreneur would be more inclined to take biased and intuitive decisions than the managers of large corporations. In uncertainty conditions these can be more efficient and innovative while managers can be more global and cautious. The over-confidence in one's self would make them more optimistic. Their capacity of representativeness, of generalizing about a person or a fact based on only a few attributes of the person or a few observations of the phenomenon, would lead them in undervalue the error and the lack of reliability of small samples. All that suggests that this type of pattern can be more adequate in company ventures and taking advantage of opportunities that do not offer sufficient information for a more rational analysis (Busenitz & Barney, 1997).

Entrepreneur and Manager therefore are complementary profiles and respond to necessities of different situations and moments. In reality both appear in the course. The "entrepreneurs" immediately take the initiative. Right from the start they take sides for determined actions, wrong or not, they organize, they are the lead players in the first cycles. Bit by bit they lose this prominence to the second profile. The numerical contents of the game become evident, the growing complexity demands method, the need of formalization or specialization is evident. Finally the "managers" are those that share leadership distributing tasks and coordinating.

When breaking down the leadership prototypes into the two previous dimensions two pairs of characteristics appear as necessary, explorer-communicator for the entrepreneur and coordinator-integrator for the manager. The combination of the four characteristics covers all the range of necessity, even though it is certain that no individual is capable of covering it all. Hence the magic of a team.

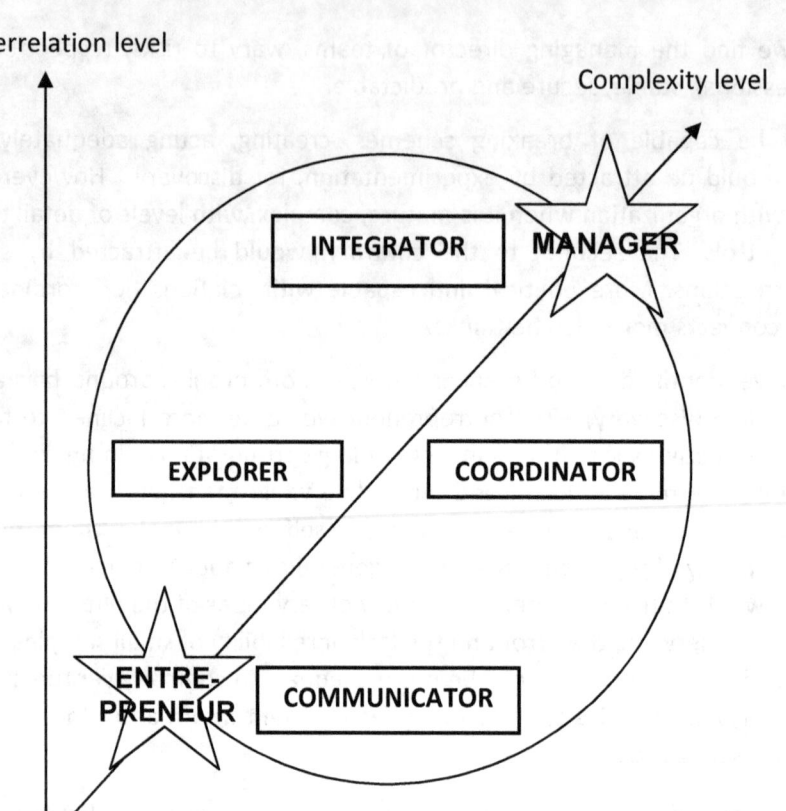

Interrelation level

Complexity level

INTEGRATOR

MANAGER

EXPLORER

COORDINATOR

ENTRE-PRENEUR

COMMUNICATOR

Interdependence level

Source: Own preparation

Illustration 8-1: Basic team leadership roles

Nevertheless it could happen that we find ourselves faced with extreme positions of roles that instead of having a positive effect on the group, collapse it confuse it or they limit its development. This happened on occasions with very strong, limiting or with participants leaderships whose level in the organization was so high that it limited the natural evolution of the group. None of these courses are included in the sample as they were considered as abnormal regarding the model. Nevertheless observing them leaves us the following proposal.

The entrepreneur at one end of the relation becomes individualist and acts as a brake, limiting and blocking the group. As this does not evolve, the manager does not even appear.

The entrepreneur at one end of the task simplifies and underestimates the potential of the simulator braking and introducing doubts about the actions of others, when they try to adopt control mechanisms or make detailed plans. He searches for the trick of the simulator convinced that if he finds it, "the" solution will depend on it. The evolution of the course overwhelms him and catches him off-foot. By when a method is clearly needed, the volume of lost information makes it impossible for them to recuperate.

The manager at the end of the relation achieves a level of integration to such a degree that the group becomes prisoner in a species of group thinking near to Groupthink (Janis, 1982)[12]. Here they cling to the less conflictive solutions rejecting criticism and even to the extreme of ignoring the interventions of the contrary participants or those that propose alternatives. The phenomenon rarely occurs at the end of the course but it has been observed half-way through, when the process of integration is at its maximum peak and the group feels that growing strength of union. At that moment the interventions, many of them correct, that involve dissidence are silenced or ignored.

The manager at one end of the task loses connection with the objective, becomes isolated and imbued by the specificities of each area of involved knowledge. The contents of the task itself becomes more important, its level of detail or its correct finalization, than the objective they are trying to achieve. His coordination task becomes obsessively centred on the task itself, losing the original sight that gave place to the specialization. This attitude does appear at the end of the course, when the there is maximum level of complexity, and normally provokes the group not finishing the planning of its action in the available time. All energy is lost along the way trying to reach a level of perfection that does not compensate the time spent on it. The results usually are that the group asks for more and more time and if it is not granted it causes them to collapse when they are in the middle of an action (game). They become incapable of making decisions having lost the reference, they become rigid and dependent of their planning and their strategy. When this fails due to "lack of time" they have no alternative or capacity for reaction. The group forgets that in complexity

---

[12] Janis empirically studied the phenomenon known as groupthink after what happened with the assessor group of President John F. Kennedy in the decision process that lead to military disasters like that of the Bay of Pigs and of the missile crisis. The groupthink members reach such a level of cohesion that any element that is potentially negative for the emotional integrity of the group is systematically denied or rejected. That includes not only the rejection of external criticism but also the cancellation of all types of self-criticism. The group selects a point of view that feeds cohesion and is self-convinced of it being the only possible solution.

there is not a sole optimal solution or that necessary investment to achieve it is not compensated with the result.

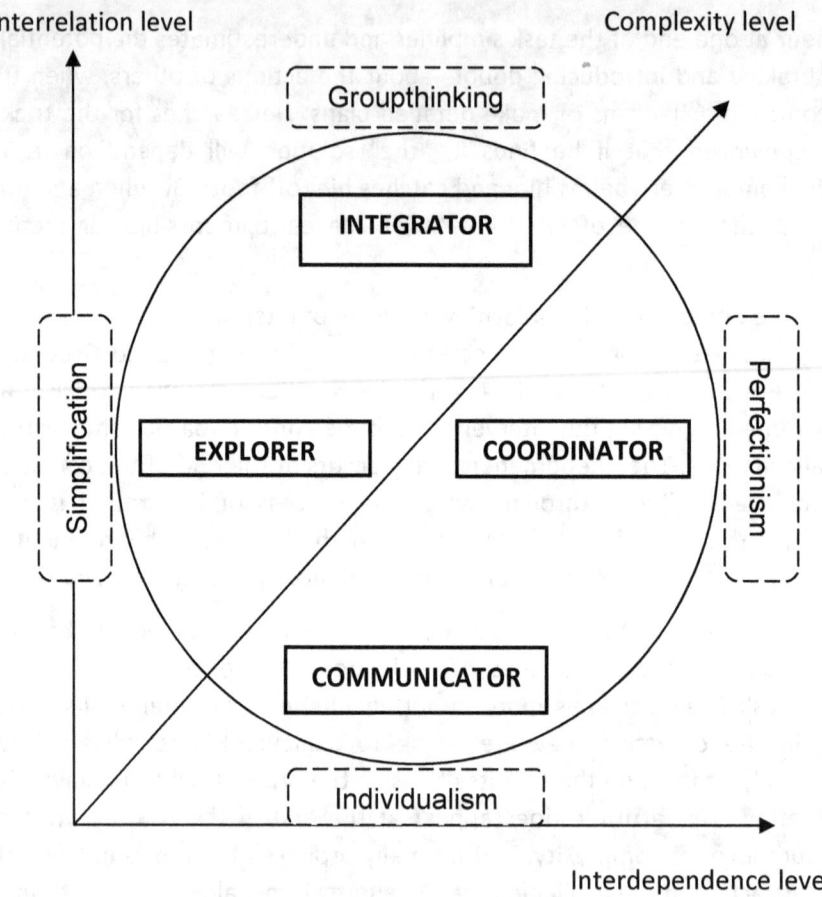

Source: Own preparation

Illustration 8-2: Team leadership roles

8.2   A Decalogue for making decisions

We remember that the course is proposed from uncertainty to complexity. The participants do not know what they are going to find and little by little they learn the basis for resolving the proposed objective. Along the way they see in interrelation and in interdependence an opportunity for obtaining synergies. Thanks to them they are capable of optimizing their investment improving their results.

During all the described process, there is a series of decisions that the group should make to be successful. I have tried to summarize in a simple way, in an easy to follow Decalogue, those steps that the most successful groups followed. That does not necessarily mean that the best groups took them all, but that they did take some or others, obtained better results at each referential moment. All together therefore they constitute a magnificent recommendation for making decisions in uncertainty and complexity.

1.   Be proactive when facing uncertainty.

The first that happens to the groups is that at the beginning and as a consequence of uncertainty they are disconcerted, lost. They make off-chance questions responding to impulses, guided more by intuition and occurrence than by a rational or analytical process. It is the first contact point. Many simply let themselves be led on, others apply the philosophy of wait and see, but others try to be proactive, have initiative, looking for agreements, etc. As McClure suggests, when facing anxiety, "The way to freedom is through the fire, not going round it" (McClure, 1998).

2.   Never lose sight of the objective.

Nevertheless, when they start to play a whole series of mental models related to the game trap them modifying the objective. They change their perception of what they want to achieve and are self-convinced about it. It is like when on Mondays we plan our week and as the week goes by we have to "put-out fires". Our strategic objective is replaced by a tactical one. If we act in the short term where we know the steps to take immediately, the level of anxiety caused by uncertainty is reduced. Nevertheless acting in the short term does not exempt from the obligation of thinking about the long term, not in vain can this modify the present up to the point of making it worthless.

3.   Use information as a base for action.

At the beginning, the groups are not usually rigorous in treating the information even when they know the uncertainty is provoked precisely by the lack of information. In part this is due to them still not being capable of structuring it and giving it meaning. At this point it is especially important to maximize and compare it.

4. Try to limit mental schemes to avoid them limiting you.

As the course advances and the groups learn the basic mechanics of the simulator, they gain confidence and become aware of the true dimension of what they are doing, of its parallelisms in the company and of its practical application. Nevertheless they are still prisoners of their mental schemes (the eye cannot see what the mind doesn't let it see), without realizing that proposed situation is new, different, and cannot be resolved using known solutions.

5. Faced with uncertainty evaluate the cost of error.

Perhaps one of the most important aspects regarding the making of decisions is the influence that the prevailing scheme of cost efficiency and scarce resources has over the group and that induces them to make gross mistakes. Faced with apparently simple decisions, they give priority to the optimization of resources and saving, with stopping to think if the resources they are saving are really scarce or if their automatic savings endanger the objective. In real life we tend to think that economic resources are scarce by definition, when really on many occasions the ideas and the opportunities are the most important. To save tangible resources they incur in unnecessary risks that frequently make the miss the objective.

Nevertheless there were groups that evaluated the cost of the error, that is, they found out what mistakes cost, to compare it with the importance of estimated savings. If making a mistake was potentially "expensive" they should allow themselves an action margin or reduce risk. Resources as such should not be an objective but rather a means to achieve it. Unfortunately, this very obvious reasoning retrospectively on occasions needs more than one mistake to appear.

6. Systematize and procedurize to advance.

The game advances and the simulator acquire its full potential. The participants know how to play, what decisions to take and start to identify fundamental relations. Something new appears on the scene then. The volume of information that they start to handle is more and larger and the inertia has driven them to the moment of pausing to allow them to think it over. The necessity of a method of capture and use of information, of organization and structuring, etc. becomes evident.

7. Facing complexity work as a team.

With multiple projects on the table, different types and quantities of resources to manage them, files and files of information, a record of previous decisions that affect the performance of the projects, dependency on other players... things get complicated. At this moment the individual capacity of understanding and managing what is happening gets less and less while the evidence of a need to work in a collective manner is more and more clear.

8. Get emotionally involved to achieve great results.

We find ourselves before a key moment for success of the group. If they manage to pass the challenge of the increase of complexity, if they manage to pass the border of individualism, if they manage at last they become cohesioned, their future possibilities of success will considerably increase. No group that has reached this point remaining in individualist positions later achieved the objective[13]. Not even those with a high technical capacity who considered they could pass the challenge, founded on the deductive logic that "should" prevail in a simulator, managed to do so. These groups forgot that the simulator is not an analytical type programmed on the base of a model but rather behavioural and therefore oriented to the stimulus of specific behaviour.

9. Grant yourself the margin of action, and foresee a contingency plan.

The final point of the history is found in front of an integrated group, with a high level of knowledge and cohesion, interchanging information, commonly and spontaneously warning each other of opportunities and risks, jointly planning. Everything seems ideal, except that too frequently, it is precisely that state of perceived security (that is commonly strengthened among them) is what on occasions fails them. If everything is clear, the alternatives are not necessary; therefore they were not even looked for. The perception of security, self-fed by the members of the team, leads to a reduction in the level of awareness and to a minimization of the evaluation of alternatives and risks.

---

[13] I remember an occasion where I was imparting a course to a management team of a large company. The President had a very dominant traditional style character. His subgroup (department), give the circumstances, just limited to following his indications. Besides he was also very competitive and thought he could always "win". Surprisingly he lost the view of that it was the company was in its entirety that should win and not one concrete player. The rest of the subgroups collaborated, among them the General Director and other first level directors. At the end of the six cycles the other subgroups achieved the objectives while the one where the President was did not. We arrived at the conclusion that his group had "sacrificed" itself for the others. The true reason of the failure did not escape the attention of anyone, not even him. In spite of the masking, the training was given and consequently they ordered more courses for the following organizational levels.

Here it is where some groups failed in spite of all the investment in time and energy in a plan that "could not fail". They forgot that the environment keeps changing although their level of expertise and confidence is high and they did not have the necessary flexibility to implement possible changes of strategy in real time. When reality came, if this did not correspond with what was planned, they did not have the capacity of reaction. A serious error in complexity, where flexibility and capacity for adaptation became very important.

10. Teamwork is not a state, it is dynamism.
    Do not allow inaction to lead you to worsening the situation.

Finally my last reflection is not referring to that observed in the course but of the level that the groups acquire. It would be a mistake to think that the level of cohesion and effectiveness that the high performance groups obtain is permanent. To the contrary it is necessary to have a policy that assures maintaining that level. Actions that are capable of maintaining the stimulus, capable of correcting a natural deterioration of relations, capable of compensating the potential worsening of the situations to which day-by-day we are led on so many occasions.

By way of a summary the Decalogue for making decisions in uncertainty and complexity says the following:

1. Be proactive when facing uncertainty.
2. Never lose sight of the objective.
3. Use information as a base for action.
4. Try to limit mental schemes to avoid them limiting you.
5. Faced with uncertainty evaluate the cost of error.
6. Systematize and procedurize to advance.
7. Facing complexity work as a team.
8. Get emotionally involved to achieve great results.
9. Grant yourself the margin of action, and foresee a contingency plan.
10. Teamwork is not a state, it is dynamism. Do not allow inaction to lead you to worsening the situation.

CHAPTER 9

CONCLUSIONS

9.1 Initial reflection

Corporate culture is the result of environments potentiated with different types of incentives and has direct consequences on the teamwork level that can be achieved. Cooperative collaborators or non-cooperative collaborators are self-chosen in the mentioned environments reinforcing the culture (Kosfeld & Siemens, 2006).

Management commitment and its active implication is fundamental to obtain an adequate environment that is capable of escalating into collaborative efforts. Company policies have to be in consonance with the objective of creating the necessary conditions for such objective.

Kosfeld and Siemens prove that in competitive markets, workers are self-selected giving place to emerging corporative cultures oriented to teamwork and to cooperation. The key mechanism is the fact that cooperative workers are capable of accepting salaries, which are lower in exchange for being separated from selfish workers. Nevertheless these latter are attracted by the high salaries and are less willing to accept other compensations different to economic ones.

Cooperative workers condition their preference to cooperate to cooperation of others. This is what is denominated "conditional cooperation". Selfish workers only respond to monetary incentives and when they do not see any economic consideration in teamwork, they never cooperate if it is not in exchange for something. Conditional cooperative workers can be stimulated both economically and non-economically.

Therefore, the existence of a whole series of incentives, where the economic factor is only a part, at the same time as teamwork stimulation by other means and the creation of the necessary conditions for its appearance, does not assure but does enormously facilitate the existence of cooperation.

Without doubt the retributive policy is one of the most important, but a similar analysis could be made with the leadership exercise, the communication and the access to information in the company, the stimulation of relations and common knowledge, recognition, the definition of responsibility levels, etc., if we want to include teamwork as one of the components of corporative culture.

9.2   Key aspects of the Cooplexity model

The model allows prescribing the behaviour of the managing teams in uncertainty and complexity circumstances. Generally speaking making decisions and management are founded on order, stability and certainty. Managers are not trained or accustomed to contend with uncertainty situations. Anxiety and bewilderment that come with such a situation are confusing and obstructing. Having a model capable of indicating a change in these situations is especially valuable in these times of crisis.

The Cooplexity model, created from the construction of an environment that allows synthesizing the behaviour essence of different management groups in exactly the same situation, something difficult to obtain in social sciences where observations cannot be isolated from the environment, proposes a work framework where we know where to start, what steps to take and what are fundamental aspects to take into consideration.

In uncertainty it is more risky to stay still than to move in the wrong direction. Proactivity, initiative and experimentation will keep us in movement, investigating, advancing and adapting ourselves. No subsystem can achieve balance in an isolated manner. Stability is reached by means of trial and error actions that permanently try to find an adequate internal configuration to the environment where one is[14].

Individual, group and team environments are not something we can unbind from each other. The three start at the same time and the three are interlocked. Some policies are not independent from others; all should have consistency among themselves in a global manner.

In spite of that, in each level of the model we will have a more emphasized approach that without losing sight of the group, allows us to concentrate on more relevant subjects for now. Knowledge, cohesion and self-coordination. This allows concentrating our efforts on a temporary sequence.

---

[14] Referring to homeostasis. Homeostasis (from the Greek word homeo that means "similar", and stasis, in Greek στάσις, "position", "stability") is the characteristic of an open system or of a closed one, especially in a live organism, by means of which the internal environment is regulated to maintain a stable and constant condition. The concept was created by Walter Bradford Cannon in 1932 (Source: Wikipedia, consulted in June, 2009).

Cohesion is by far the most important level of all. Considered as a key variable by the majority of scholars of this subject, it is a necessary requirement so that the third level can be achieved.

Self-coordination, the authentic artificer of efficiency, becomes centralized coordination without cohesion, losing all its attributes and with that its efficiency.

Self-coordination and especially the emergence, varies the traditional approach of management as a series of actions and decisions about the group and it focuses it on a series of actions and decisions about the environment. Creating adequate conditions facilitating emergence instead of forcing determined actions is fundamental in the model.

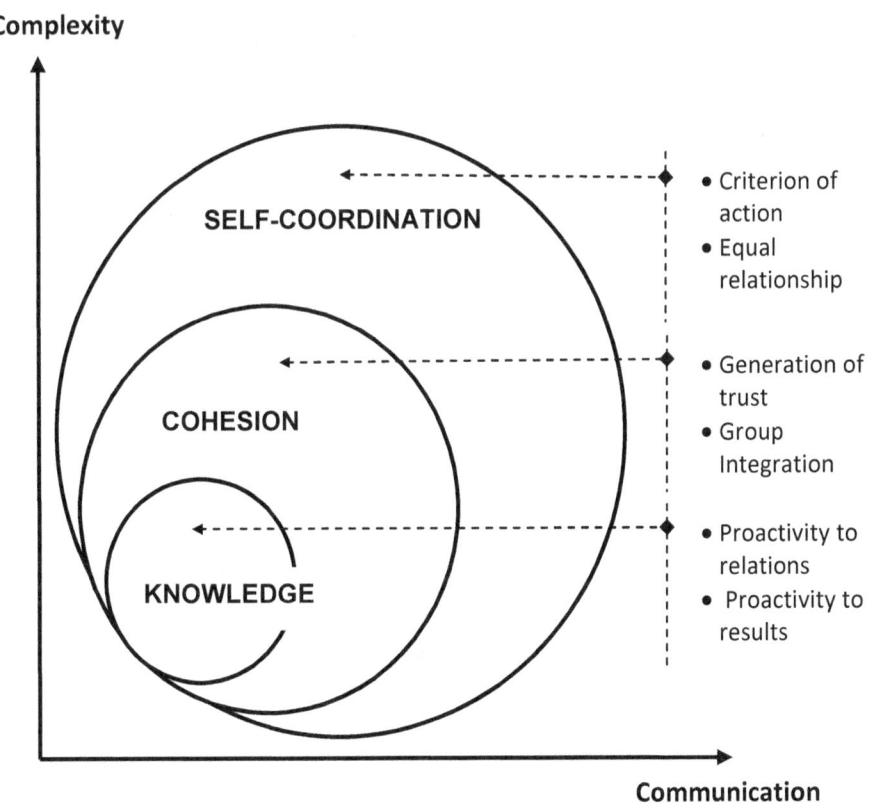

9.3 Collaboration is not always possible

Three levels of collaboration are clearly observed in the groups according to the moment they happen and the three have different implications. With the first that I identify as the Alliance everybody wins and nobody loses. The agreement is obvious and nobody rejects it. As soon as an opportunity for collaboration under these circumstances appears it is accepted.

While the group evolves and the integration process follows it course, new opportunities for cooperation, that although not harming anyone, do create unequal benefits. Here is where the group usually reaches agreements that produced benefit is attributed to one's self earlier or later as compensation or reciprocity. It is the interchange level or *Cooperation*. In day-to-day reality we could consider that the win-win negotiations are located here. A value and according compensations are negotiated. The level of cooperation is not a bad one although we can still consider that it produces optimal results for the group.

Global necessities are attended in the third level at the same time as individual ones, but contemplating the group as a whole, as a system, as an entity with its own differentiating personality and particularities. That way its members feel that they have made an important qualitative jump. This is the *Collaboration* level.

When reaching this point it becomes necessary to make an essential distinction between cooperation and collaboration. Cooperation is linear, concrete, oriented to an objective. In cooperative work the tasks are subdivided between the members and which one works separately. Coordination is important in terms of who does what, how and when (Nezamirad, Higgins, & Dunstall, 2005).

Collaboration is a creative process between two or more persons, with complementary abilities that interact to create a common understanding that nobody previously had and would not have been able to acquire alone. Collaboration creates common contents about a process, a product, or an event. In this sense, there is nothing routinized. This is something that did not previously exist (Schrage, 1990).

Collaboration is a state that has many components and one of them is cooperation. Cooperation also is about a common purpose but at a lower abstraction level, more operative. Collaboration is a creative process where the result is the emerging product as a consequence of interaction. If cooperation needs coordination, collaboration needs self-coordination.

If we place the three level of collaboration in accord to the achieved team conscience we would have a scheme like the following.

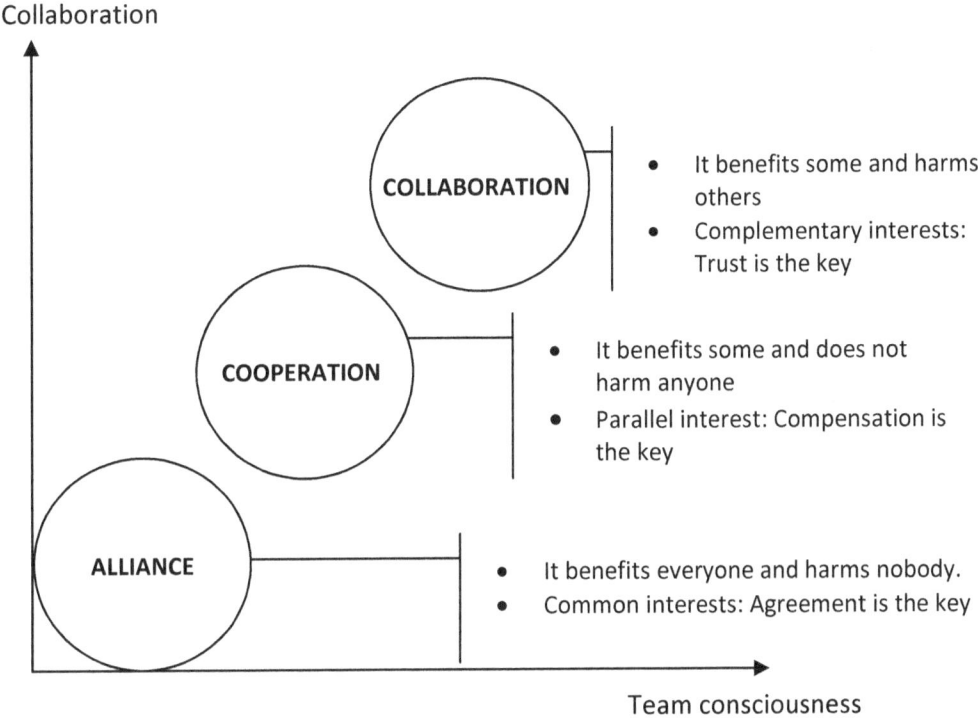

Illustration 9-1: The three possible collaboration levels

Trust is very important in the last level as we assure that although actions apparently contrary to individual interests exist, these decisions will not be judged as transgressions or aggressions but rather as a search for common benefit that includes the individual that takes it into account and finally balances it.

In the Collaboration level the individual and common objectives lose their differentiation. They should be achieved together and in a balanced manner. Going to the other extreme, that the group "only" thinks of a group is not positive, it should also think of the individual. Like as in a company, the dichotomy is proposed among the objectives in a clear manner from a conceptual point of view but hardly defined from an operational point of view. To go after one's own interest is only logical; to do it only with attention placed on common interest (even at the expense of the individual) is also logical. The problem lies in reconciling both objectives in a balanced manner. Unfortunately here, as in the majority of complexity situations, there are no recipes.

Neither more nor less it is a case of obtaining balance between individual and global interests.

Curiously when the group is integrated, it is perfectly capable of understanding it and achieving it, but it is very important that it does, as we are in the final process of evolution. Previously, any attempt to achieve common benefit by the more collaborative participants is rejected when considering that individual benefit is at risk. To be collaborative in the long term, the individuals should also achieve their individual objectives or have a reasonable expectation that the cost of collaboration will be compensated earlier or later.

When the agents or not interdependent, survival is reduce to win-lose competition, where the strongest individual survives. However in complexity this is not applicable. Interrelations and interdependencies cause the most selfish decision to be precisely the most collaborative. Not only that, the interested use of resources with the sole aim of obtaining individual yields will be rejected by the group. On occasions, decisions taken in this direction were identified in the groups, with disastrous results for the cohesion and regressions to previous more individualist positions. These groups could have obtained worse results after a crisis than those obtained in previous game cycles.

Somebody could think that those who only intermediate for their own interests are more selfish or interested. On occasions, this assumption may not be totally right. The degree of collaboration observed in the groups was directly related with the level of trust and therefore with the perceived level of risk. There is a natural tendency in all human beings that pushes them to survival. Therefore perceiving risk releases a series of self-protection mechanisms that push one to take-up more individualist positions. In the measure that the group increases the level of trust among its members and reduces in parallel the perceived risk of the decisions it takes, it becomes more capable of showing collaborative attitudes. Therefore the trick consists of regulating the key to trust and risk to allow the appearance of such decisions.

Robert Axelrod in his work The Evolution of Cooperation contributes some keys that we can perfectly recompile here. Using the famous game "The Prisoner's Dilemma" created around 1950 by Merrill Flood and Melvin Dresher and later formalized with its current name by A.W. Tucker, Axelrod invited experts in game theory to a tournament. The competition consisted in sending programs in which the participant should choose between making a cooperative decision or a non-cooperative one faced with a series of repeated interactions of the game. Among them all, the strategy called "Tit For Tat" from Professor Anatol Rapoport of the Toronto University always won. What was surprising is that its strategy was also the most simple. It consisted in that the first decision was always cooperative while after it systematically repeated the decision of its opponent (Axelrod, 1984).

As in the Tit For Tat strategy, that group that initiated its activity in a corporative manner, that is giving the system and opportunity, advances more and goes further in the processes of the model. Likewise the reciprocity concept, a key on in the Axelrod work was like a consequence of complementarity of the interests of the group, of its capacity to reject cooperation if the expectation of returns did not exist and of the real and close perception that the cooperative effort would be compensated. That way one would be cooperative of the other party was also and would generate common benefit. To the contrary, this would not be so if the other weren't.

When extrapolating these teachings to the reality of groups, therefore we have to take into account that the size of these play against the perception of individual contribution and the expectation of returns. In addition, it would be a negative factor if the benefit of cooperative effort were unequally shared among the members giving way to a less clear expectation of reciprocity. When designing teams and compensatory policies, thus it would be necessary to divide large group into smaller teams to improve this perception.

By integrating collaboration levels in the model, we observe that the Alliance level is accessible to any series of individuals with coinciding interests. The level of cooperation would be at the reach of those groups that have initiated integration processes and have minimum trust, sufficient to sustain the negotiating process and the establishment of compensations on equal terms. When the minimum level of trust is missing negotiation cannot progress even though both parties consider a potential agreement as beneficial. Finally the maximum level of collaboration forcedly needs to be situated at the highest level of the model.

9.4 Implications

The Cooplexity model has management implications that due to their extension cannot be covered in this summary and that are the object of the book of the same title (see www.traininggames.com). Among them I will mention the collaboration objective that is reasonable expected at each level, the leadership roles that have to allow the evolution of the group into a team, the impact of the uncertainty in management, the analysis of all the decisions, the relation with what has been called Group Emotional Intelligence and the parallelisms with Distributed Leadership.

Another series of repercussions will be related to the intrinsically necessary aspects for the correct development of the model like delegation, levels of responsibility in the positions, tolerance of errors, handling of information, etc.

Finally there is a whole series of more or less important findings from the original study and the final model among which the following are outstanding:

a. Teamwork alone is not a universal solution or an objective.

b. The excess of cohesion is a disadvantage.

c. Teamwork is an emerging pattern

d. Teamwork is decentralized

e. Equality is an element that limits performance.

f. Teamwork is not an individual competence

INDEX OF ILLUSTRATIONS AND TABLES

INDEX OF ILUSTRATIONS

INDEX OF TABLES

BIBLIOGRAPHY

Adams, J. S. (1965). Inequity in Social Exchange. (L. Berkowitz, Ed.) *Advances in Experimental Social Psychology* , 267-300.

Axelrod, R. (1984). *The Evolution of Cooperation.* New York: Basic Books.

Belbin, R. M. (1981). *Management Teams. Why they succeed or fail.* London: William Heinemann Ltd.

Belbin, R. M. (1993). *Team Roles at Work.* London: William Heinemann Ltd.

Bennis, W. G., & Shepard, H. A. (1956). A Theory of Group Development. *Human Relations , 9* (4), 415.

Bion, W. R. (1991). *Experiences in Groups and Other Papers.* London: Routledge.

Boyatzis, R. E. (1982). *The Competence Manager. A model for Effective Performance.* USA: John Wiley & Sons.

Busenitz, L. W., & Barney, J. B. (1997). Differences between entrepreneurs and managers in large organizations: Biases and heuristics in strategic decision-making. *Journal of Business Venturing* (12), 9-30.

Carron, A. V., & Hausenblas, H. A. (1998). *Group dynamics in sport* (2 ed.). Morgantown WV: Fitness Information Technology.

Carron, A. V., Brawley, L. R., & Widmeyer, W. N. (1998). The measurement of cohesiveness in sport groups. En J. L. Duda (Ed.), *Advances in sport and exercise psychology measurements* (págs. 213-226). Morgantown WV: Fitness Information Technology.

Crant, M. J. (2000). Proactive Behavior in Organizations. *Journal of Management , 26* (3), 435-462.

Drexler, A. B., Sibbet, D., & Forrester, R. H. (1988). The Team Performance Model. En W. B. Reddy, & K. Jamison (Edits.), *Team building: Blueprints for productivity and satisfaction* (págs. 45-61). San Diego: NTL Institute for Applied Behavioral Science.

Druskat, V. U., & Wolff, S. B. (2005). Inteligencia Emocional Grupal y su Influencia en la Efectividad del Grupo. En D. Goleman, & C. Cherniss (Edits.), *Inteligencia Emocional en el Trabajo* (M. Portillo, Trad., págs. 203-230). Barcelona: Kairós.

Festinger, L., Schacter, S., & Back, K. (1950). *Social Pressures in Informal Groups.* Stanford, CA: Stanford University Press.

Forrester, J. W. (1961). *Industrial dynamics.* Waltham, MA: Pegasus Communications.

Hosmer, L. T. (1995). Trust: The Connecting Link between Organizational Theory and Philosophical Ethics. *The Academy of Management Review , 20* (2), 379-403.

Janis, I. L. (1982). *Groupthink. Psychological studies of policy decisions and fiascoes.* Boston, MA: Houghton Mifflin.

Katzenbach, J. R., & Smith, D. K. (1992). *The Wisdom of Teams: Creating the High Performance Organization.* Boston MA: Harvard Business School Press.

Kosfeld, M., & Siemens, F. (2006). *Competition, Cooperation, and Corporate Culture.* Paper, University of Zurich, Foundations of Human Social, Behavior: Altruism versus Egoism.

Lakin, M. (1972). *Interpersonal Encounter: Theory and Practice in Sensitivity Training.* New York: McGraw-Hill.

Margerison, C., & McCann, D. (1990). *Team Management, Practical new approaches.* London: Mercury Books.

McClelland, D. C. (1973). Testing for competence rather than for intelligence. *American Psychologist* (28), 1-14.

McClure, B. A. (1998). *Putting a New Spin on Groups: The Science of Chaos.* Mahwah, NJ: Lawrence Erlbaum.

Moreland, R. L., & Levine, J. M. (2006). Socialization in Organizations and Work Groups. En R. L. Moreland, & J. M. Levine (Edits.), *Smal Groups* (págs. 469-498). New York, NY: Psychology Press.

Munné, F. (1999). Constructivismo, construccionismo y complejidad: la debilidad de la crítica en la psicología construccional. *Revista de Psicología Social , 14* (2-3), 131-144.

Nezamirad, K., Higgins, P. G., & Dunstall, S. (2005). Human collaboration in planning and scheduling. En *7th International Workshop on Human Factors in Planning, Scheduling and Control in Manufacturing.* The Netherlands: The University of Groningen.

Robbins, S. P. (1999). *Comportamiento Organizacional* (8 ed.). Mexico: Prentice Hall.

Saunders, D., & Powell, T. (1998). Developing a European media simulation through new information and communication technologies: The TENSAL project. En J. Rolfe, D. Saunders, & T. Powell (Edits.), *The International Simulation & Gaming Research Yearbook. Simulations and Games for Emergency and Crisis Management* (Vol. 6, págs. 75-86). London: Kogan Page.

Schein, E. H. (2004). *Organizational Culture and Leadership* (3 ed.). San Francisco: Jossey-Bass.

Schrage, M. (1990). *Shared Minds: The New Technologies of Collaboration.* Baltimore, MD, U.S.A.: Random House.

Senge, P. M. (1990). *The Fifth Discipline: The Art and practice of the learning organizations.* New York: Doubleday.

Simon, H. A. (1997). *Administrative Behavior. A study of decision-making processes in administrative organizations.* (4 ed.). New York, NY: The Free Pres.

Sitkin, S. B. (1995). Learning through failure: The strategy of small losses. En M. D. Cohen, & L. S. Sproull (Edits.), *Organizational Learning* (págs. 541-578). Thousand Oaks, CA: Sage.

Spencer, L. M., & Spencer, S. M. (1993). *Competence at Work: Models for Superior Performance.* USA: John Wiley & Sons.

Tsuchiya, T., & Tsuchiya, S. (1999). The unique contribution of gaming/simulation: towards establishment of the discipline. En D. Saunders, & J. Severn (Edits.), *The International Simulation & Gaming Research Yearbook. Simulations and Games for Strategy and Planning* (Vol. 7, págs. 46-57). London: Kogan Page.

Tuckman, B. W. (1965). Developmental sequences in small groups. *Psychological Bulletin* (63), 384-399.

Tuckman, B. W., & Jensen, M. A. (1977). Stages of small group development revisited. *Group and Organizational Studies* (2), 419-427.

REFERENCES

"participate in SYNERGY meant an intellectual challenge due to the different way of approaching a well-known subject. The idea of breaking schemes and not being anchored to traditional ones became perfectly clear. Learning to dominate any natural leadership to adapt it to good teamwork was another good practice."

"On the whole an intense and very recommendable experience for those that want to learn with different methodologies."

Jordi Ballesté
Managing Director
Grupo Angelini

"The configuration of a new Team of people coming from different business areas and even from other organizations, with the aim of taking on a large project, motivated the necessity of developing a training program that would facilitate interpersonal knowledge and promote teamwork. Above all, it was necessary to establish the challenges and problems, which we face, this more innovative aspect in what regards a training activity. The experience with the Balance Cone was at the same time, rewarding and successful, as it conjugated playing aspects (games and simulators) and operational ones (specific work projects) that brought satisfaction to the objectives, both in cohesion as in efficiency, respectively."

Ricardo Alonso Fernández
Director of Corporate Banking
Global Banking & Markets
Banco Santander

"SYNERGY is an intelligent way of demonstrating by play that in a company we are all necessary and that union is strength. It is a song to transversatility and in Dannon it has been very useful to become aware of the importance that people have in all functions, each one in their role, so that projects advance and become realities."

Robert Cosialls
Purchasing Director of South Europe
Dannon

"Without doubt it is a professional and well organized game. It creates initiative and excitement in the participants with being too competitive. It helps to form teams and helps the participant to obtain the effect. Ahah! I mean that, of course, everyone knows that collaboration is important and of course, everyone knows that we should trust one another but this exercise helps people to really experience it. I think that the game can cover a large variety of learning objectives such as teamwork, collaboration, team building, etc."

Jeff Tomlinson
Director of Production
HEINEKEN

"A few years ago I met Ricardo Zamora. He presented to us a teamwork project that we would like. The truth is due it being innovative and atypical, I have to confess, that after the presentation mi initial idea was to forget the whole thing. Nevertheless, we though it over and decided to send an elite group to receive this training. It was an outstanding success, a total innovation in our training system, and most of all, that the team enjoyed it and admitted having learned such important subjects like, communication, teamwork, works systems, etc. During these last three years, all our team of managers and middle-managers, with excellent results when it comes to applying the acquired knowledge in their day-to-day work."

Antonio Mateo Navarro
Director of Industrial Relations and Training
Lafarge

"It has meant a magnificent personal experience for me and all my team in which, by means of the innovative inductive and active methodology, in which starting from individual knowledge and experience, developed through game or simulation techniques, we have acquired training by discovery that is strongly consolidated as a fruit of our own experience, obtaining an immediate and inevitable transfer of that training to our professional work as a team, and always looking for ways to apply it day-to-day."

José Poch Riba
General Manager Automotive Foam Division
Grupo Copo

ABOUT THE AUTHOR

Ricardo Zamora Enciso is Bachelor and Master of Science in Business Administration by ESADE (Top 10 European and International Business Schools, www.esade.edu).

He is associate professor at ESADE Business School - Executive Education, Department of Business Policy since 2000

In 1995 he founded Training Games (www.traininggames.com); a training consultancy specialized in Simulation & Gaming, that is to say, in the application of active pedagogy to learning. He is the creator of simulators like Synergy, Carterbanc or Salesmanship and games like Teaching cards, Fork, The 5 phases of sales and Linker.

He is the founder of the Cooplexity Institute (www.cooplexity.com), focused on making know the Cooplexity model, a model of cooperation in complexity to manage interrelations and interdependences under uncertainty and changing environments.

He has become specialized in teams, an area to which he currently dedicates all his research efforts. He is member of the ESADE's Leadership Development Research Centre focused on effective leadership and emotional and social competencies (Glead).

Some of his clients are Arbora & Ausonia (Procter & Gamble), Grupo Santander, Deutsche Bank, Lafarge, Heineken, Nestlé, Dannon, Nabisco, BDF-Biedersdorf, HP, Akzo Nobel, Unilever, BASF or Solvay among others. He also collaborates in the public sector with the different institutions from national to local levels.

He is a member of the System Dynamics Society and NASAGA (North American Simulation and Gaming Association).

TO KNOW MORE

Ricardo Zamora Enciso has a blog for discussion about the subjects related with this book at: www.ricardozamora.com

If you wish to obtain the original work: "Cooplexity. A model of collaboration in complexity for management in times of uncertainty and change. http://stores.lulu.com/RicardoZamora

Face up to the crisis, permanent change, uncertainty, is something more than organizations should collectively do from a team and distributed leadership point of view.

Cooplexity proposes a cooperation-collaboration model in complexity which is the result of more than ten years research and five gathering data. Three action levels are rigorously proposed, their implications, their key factors and the catalyzers that have allowed them to appear.

All the research has been carried out based on the behaviours observed in management teams interacting in Synergy, a training course that structured around a behavioural simulator takes the participants from an environment of uncertainty to one of complexity.

The reader will find in this book the guidelines to facilitate the emergency of collaborative behaviours as well as series of conclusions that challenge the classic concepts of team work and of leadership as they have been understood until now.

www.ingramcontent.com/pod-product-compliance
Lightning Source LLC
Chambersburg PA
CBHW081215170526
45165CB00009B/2826